PASS YOUR DRIVING TEST FIRST TIME!

PASS YOUR DRIVING TEST FIRST TIME!

Text by Mike Gilhespy

Illustrated by Adrian Deadman

Published in association with The British School of Motoring Ltd

First published in the UK in 1990 by
New Holland (Publishers) Ltd
37 Connaught Street, London W2 2AZ

Second edition 1990 (reprinted 1991)

Third edition (revised and updated) 1992, reprinted 1992, 1993

ISBN   1 85368 202 0 (pbk)
        1 85368 131 8 (hbk)

Commissioning editor: Charlotte Parry-Crooke
Editors: Ann Baggaley, Maggi McCormick
Design: ML Design
Cover design: Adrian Deadman

Typeset by ML Design
Reproduction by Scantrans Pte Ltd, Singapore
Printed and bound in Singapore by Kyodo Printing Co (Singapore) Pte Ltd

The traffic signs on pages 52-5 and 79 are reproduced by
kind permission of Her Majesty's Stationery Office.

Contents

Foreword

In today's world most people need to use a car, so being able to drive is almost an essential skill. What is also essential, of course, is safe, thoughtful driving practice – good habits, learned at an early stage, will benefit you for a lifetime of driving. So it is always worth the time and effort of learning to drive properly, whether you intend to use your car for work or leisure.

I ran The British School of Motoring for nearly twenty years and had always wanted to be involved with the production of a *really* useful – and approachable – book on learning to drive. *Pass Your Driving Test First Time!* is the result both of that long-held ambition and of the experience and knowledge gained over many years of developing the most effective methods of teaching people to drive safely and surely.

Of course, there is no substitute for practical experience and the best way to gain this is to have tuition with a good professional driving instructor. However, this book *can* make learning easier, and your lessons more effective, by preparing you for each stage and reminding you of what you have been taught. It not only takes you through the first steps of mastering the controls of the car but it also prepares you for the test itself – a milestone in any driver's career. And it will continue to be a useful companion after the test, seeing you onto the road as a 'solo' driver as opposed to leaving you either wondering what to do next or making the assumption that you have nothing further to learn. (You go on learning every time you get into the driving seat of a car, I assure you!)

The design is lively and inviting, and the illustrations, picture questions and quizzes are informative and entertaining; above all, the advice is eminently sound and practical. I feel sure that this book will encourage and help you to approach learning to drive without trepidation, to pass the test with confidence and, most importantly, to drive safely and effectively for the rest of your driving career.

Good luck – and pass first time!

Sir Anthony Jacobs
Chairman 1973-1990
The British School of Motoring Ltd

Introduction

For most of us, learning to drive means passing the Driving Standards Agency Test. We want to achieve the freedom of travel that a full driving licence bestows. That moment when we receive our 'Pass Certificate' and can tear up the 'L' plates is a time of extraordinary joy and relief. Grown men burst into tears and old ladies kiss their examiners.

Sadly, only about 50 per cent of all driving tests conducted result in a pass, which is frustrating for examiners and candidates alike. There are as many tears of sadness as of joy. If you have started, or are about to start to learn to drive, you should recognise that this is a most important time in your life. If you want to be successful, you need to give a lot of thought as to how best to achieve your aim.

This book has been designed to help you. Its colourful step-by-step approach makes learning easy, and forms an excellent preparation programme for the driving test. Because it illustrates the habits you need to acquire to be a safe driver, the book also sets you on the right road to improving your skills after the test and surviving and remaining accident-free on today's busy roads.

Preparing for your test
The first section of the book explains how to get started, obtain a licence, plan your practice and lessons and prepare for your test. It also explains what happens on the day of the test itself.

What the examiner is testing
There are 21 items on which you may be tested; this book takes you step by step through each one. Correct procedures, common faults and tips on how to improve are all explained.

Theoretical driving tests
As well as asking you to perform the practical exercises, the examiner will ask you questions about the Highway Code and 'other motoring matters'. On pages 56-63 a series of traffic situations is presented in picture form so that you can test your understanding of the rules of the road, road signs and road surface markings and car control. You will also find quizzes in this book, designed to test your knowledge of the road signs from the Highway Code and to help you answer some of those awkward questions about things such as tyres and skidding and simple car mechanics — things that most learners dread being asked.

After the test
This section explains what happens when you pass or fail the test, and gives advice on what to do next.

Driving on your own

When you have passed your test, you will still have much to learn. There are sections which look at the basics of:

- Safe motorway driving.
- Safe night driving.
- Car maintenance.

The look and learn method

To make learning with this book more enjoyable and to help you remember what you have learnt, many drawings have been used. By studying the diagrams and their accompanying explanations, you will be able to understand easily the essential points and procedures you need to know to pass your driving test. The cartoon-style pictures will, we hope, entertain you – but, more importantly, they are intended to help you remember the rules you must learn and the faults you must avoid.

The need for a professional driving instructor

The Driving Standards Agency strongly recommends that you take lessons from an Approved Driving Instructor. There is no doubt that this is both the best and safest way to learn. Any person who gives car driving lessons for payment or reward must be registered with the Driving Standards Agency. He or she is required to display an ADI identification certificate on the windscreen of the tuition car. To become an ADI, you must pass examinations which are of a high standard.

Developing your driving skills

If you study this book carefully, you will certainly improve your chances of passing your driving test first time. You should learn more quickly, because you will understand better what your instructor explains to you.

We hope you will also begin a lifelong interest in developing your driving skills. Driving can be a great pleasure, but also a great risk. Skilled drivers understand both the pleasure and the risks, and show by every action they take that they care for their own and other people's safety.

Over 5,000 people are killed on our roads each year. About 250,000 are seriously injured. Nearly all these deaths and injuries are the result of driver error and could be avoided. Nobody expects to have an accident, and nor will you. If you care about people, you will make that expectation a reality and remain accident free.

Good luck.

Preparing for learning to drive

The legal requirements

The minimum age at which you are normally allowed to drive a car on the public roads is 17. If you are a disabled person and in receipt of mobility allowance, the minimum age is 16. Until you have passed your driving test you must be accompanied by a person who is over 21 years of age and who has held a full British driving licence, valid for the type of vehicle you wish to drive, for a minimum of three years.

(1)   *Do not put 'L' plates in the windows where they will restrict your vision.*

(2)   *Heavy boots or high heels make it hard to feel and control the pedals.*

Before you drive, you must obtain a provisional driving licence. You can get an application form, D1, from any Post Office. You must not drive until you have received this first licence and have signed it in ink.

Before you drive you must make sure your eyesight meets the minimum standard (page 12).

You must check that any vehicle you drive is taxed. The tax disc must be displayed on the nearside (left) corner of the windscreen.

You must check that the vehicle is insured for you to drive and to learn in. If the vehicle is more than three years old, check that it has an MOT Test Certificate.

You must fix 'L' plates of the regulation size to the vehicle so that they are visible from front and rear. Do not put 'L' plates in the windows where they will restrict your vision (1).

Personal preparation

There are many things that your instructor will need to explain to you about driving. You will save considerable time on your lessons, and are likely to learn more quickly if you read the Highway Code before you start to drive.

When you start to have lessons, make sure that you wear comfortable shoes. Heavy boots or high heels (2) make it hard to feel and control the pedals.

Applying for your driving test

The purpose of the driving test is to find out whether you can drive safely, without supervision, on the roads. You will not pass unless you can show the examiner that you have this ability.

Most people find it best to apply for the test as soon as they start having lessons. This gives a goal to aim for and encourages you to keep learning. The number of lessons and amount of practice you have each week will obviously affect how long it will take to reach the required standard. You should discuss this with your driving instructor, who can then advise you about requesting an appropriate test date. If you do not progress as quickly as you had hoped, your instructor will advise you to postpone the test date. You should take this advice, as you will waste your money if you take the test before you are ready. Provided you give 10 clear working days' notice, you can cancel your test appointment and book another date without losing the fee.

To apply for your test, you need to get a form DL26, which is available from Post Offices and Regional Driving Standards Agency Offices. The completed form and fee should be sent to the appropriate Regional Office. You will find the address on the form. After about two weeks, you will receive a form DL28, which is your test appointment card. Make sure you show this card to your instructor and keep it somewhere safe.

The driving test

Your driving test will last about 35 minutes, and will include an eyesight test, general driving, special exercises and questions on the Highway Code and other motoring matters.

There are 21 specific items on which the examiner may test you. Each one is explained on pages 12-55 of this book. As listed by the Driving Standards Agency they are:

1. Eyesight test.
2. Highway Code.
3. Checks before starting the engine.
4. Using the controls.
5. Moving away.
6. Emergency stop.
7. Reversing.
8. Turning in the road.
9. Reverse parking.
10. Using the mirrors.
11. Giving signals.
12. Acting on signs and signals.
13. Care in the use of speed.
14. Making progress.
15. Road junctions (including roundabouts).
16. Overtaking, meeting and crossing the path of other vehicles.
17. Position on the road.
18. Passing stationary vehicles.
19. Pedestrian crossings.
20. Selecting a safe position for normal stops.
21. Awareness and anticipation.

The day of your test

You should bring your test appointment card and, if you are not taking the test in a driving school car, your insurance certificate. You must also bring your driving licence or some other acceptable proof of your identity, such as a passport or an identity card issued by your employer which bears your name, photograph and signature. Make sure your car is clean and in good working order (3).

Arrive in plenty of time (4). Be warned: some test centres do not have toilets.

You will wait in the waiting room, and probably feel very nervous. Your instructor will try to help by keeping you occupied until the test begins.

The examiner will appear, call out your name, ask you to sign against your name and also to show proof of your identity. (If you cannot prove who you are, your test may be cancelled and you will lose your fee.) He will then ask you to lead the way to your vehicle. You will probably be pleasantly surprised to find that he is a friendly, human-looking individual (5) and your confidence will rise.

The examiner will ask which car is yours, and then ask you to read a car number plate (see page 12). Your driving test will have begun. What happens when it is all over is explained on page 68.

(3)   *Make sure your car is clean and in good working order.*

(4)   *Arrive in plenty of time. Be warned: some test centres do not have toilets.*

(5)   *Examiners are human after all.*

Eyesight test

(1) *The examiner will ask you to read a car number plate.*

Good eyesight is essential for safe driving. You must be able to read a car number plate from a distance of 20.5 metres (67 feet). You are allowed to wear glasses or contact lenses if necessary, but if you have any doubts about your ability to meet the eyesight requirements easily, seek advice from an optician before you take the test.

Most people are able to detect movement to the left and right without moving their heads. This is called your 'field of vision' and is normally 180° . Some people suffer from a severely restricted field of vision, which is referred to as 'tunnel vision'. People with tunnel vision can see only a little to the left or right without moving their heads. If you suffer from this problem, you should seek advice from an optician.

Some people are colour-blind. This disability does not stop you from driving, but you should make sure that your driving instructor is aware of your problem. He will want to be extra sure that you can recognise road signs by their shapes and understand the sequence of lights at traffic signals and pelican crossings, as this is more difficult without the colour to help you.

It is illegal to drive a car if you cannot pass the eyesight test.

Soon after leaving the waiting room at the beginning of your test, the examiner will ask you to read a car number plate (1).

He will pick a distance further away than the minimum 20.5 metres. If you cannot read it he will move closer to another plate. If you still have problems, he will use a tape measure to mark out the exact distance of 20.5 metres to another number plate.

If you still cannot read it, you will fail the test, and will not be asked to drive.

Remember, if you wear glasses or contact lenses to read the number plate, you must continue to wear them the whole of the time you are driving.

It makes sense to have your eyesight checked regularly by an optician. The chart below shows the usual distance test, in which letters of graded sizes are viewed.

A C E H
T L C N O
O D E C L

Do:

• Check your eyesight before you start to drive.

• Consult an optician if in doubt.

• If you wear glasses normally, always wear them when driving.

Don't:

• Wait until the day of your test to find that your eyesight is inadequate.

Checks before starting the engine

(1) *Check that the doors are closed.*

When you get into your car, you should check that:

• The doors are properly closed (1).

• The seat is adjusted so that you can reach the controls easily without stretching (2).

• The interior and door mirrors are adjusted to give the best possible view (3). You should not have to move your head in order to see in the interior mirror.

• Your seat belt is fastened (4).

Before you start the engine, make sure that the handbrake is on and that the gear lever is in neutral.

If the car is in gear, it will lurch away as you turn the key to start the engine.

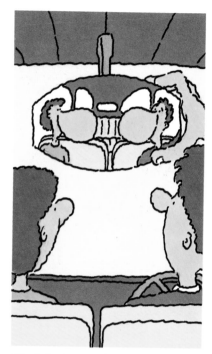

(3) *Adjust your mirrors.*

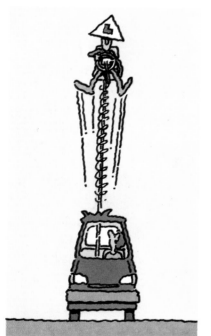

(2) *Adjust your seat.*

Do:

• Make these safety checks a habit.

Don't:

• Adjust your interior mirror for the day of your test so that you have to move your head to see in it. The examiner is trained to see if you move only your eyes, not your whole head, in order to look in the mirrors.

(4) *Fasten your seat belt.*

Using the controls

When you take your driving test, the examiner will be looking to see that you are in full control of your vehicle at all times. You will need to be able to use all the controls smoothly, correctly and at the right time.

Steering
Steering a steady course along the road has much to do with how you use your eyes.

Don't look down at the end of the bonnet, as this tends to make you weave from one side of the road to the other.

Looking well ahead helps keep the car in a straight line (1). So keep your head up and your eyes high.

Keep both hands on the steering wheel (2). Position them at ten to two, or a quarter to three.

Remember, it is normally only the front wheels that steer. When you turn left, the back wheels cut in (3) and will mount the kerb if you steer too early.

When turning right, you will cut the corner if you steer too early (4).

The handbrake
The purpose of the handbrake is to hold the car still when you are stopped or parked. It normally works only on the two rear wheels. Don't use the handbrake to stop the car. You may skid, or even cause the car to spin round.

The accelerator
Using the accelerator is one way of controlling the speed of the car. The pedal is very sensitive, so make gentle changes of pressure on it (5). Sudden movements up or down may cause the car to jolt.

You need to balance the accelerator and clutch to make a smooth start.

(3) *The back wheels cut in when turning left.*

(1) *Look well ahead.*

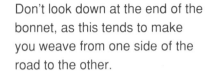

(4) *Don't cut right-hand corners.*

(2) *Keep both hands on the steering wheel.*

(5) *Be gentle with the accelerator.*

The footbrake

The footbrake is the other main way of controlling the speed of the car. Its purpose is to help you slow down or stop. In normal driving, only light pressure is needed on the pedal to brake safely and smoothly.

Harsh braking gives a rough ride, and may cause you to skid (6). Early braking allows more time for drivers behind you to see your brake lights, and reduces the risk of someone bashing into the rear end of your car.

The clutch and clutch control

When you are stationary, the clutch allows the engine to keep running without driving the wheels. With a gear engaged, as you let the clutch pedal up, you reach a point where the engine starts to turn the wheels. This is called the 'biting point'. To move off smoothly, you need to let the clutch pedal up to the biting point and then keep your feet still on both the accelerator and clutch pedals. Sudden movements will cause a jerky start, and may cause the engine to stall. Tiny movements of the clutch pedal will make the car speed up or slow down.

The ability to find the biting point, and to control the speed of the car's movement in this way, is what is meant by clutch control. It is essential when moving off, and also when manoeuvring in confined spaces where you wish the car to creep along at less than walking pace.

Push down the clutch every time you change gear.

Push down the clutch just before you stop. If you forget, the engine will stall.

Do not drive along with your foot resting on the clutch pedal (7). This wears it out very quickly.

The gears

The gears enable you to match the power of the engine to both the speed of the car and the effort needed to keep it moving.

Low gears give a lot of power but little speed. High gears give less power but more speed (8). To change gear smoothly requires practice, because you need to co-ordinate the clutch and accelerator carefully.

Knowing when to change gear involves making judgements about your car's capabilities, your speed and the road and traffic conditions.

Do not look down at the controls when changing gear.

Do not coast, by allowing the car to run on in neutral, or with the clutch pedal down.

To pass your driving test, and to be a safe driver, you must be in full control of your car at all times. You can only achieve this skill through practice.

(6) *Harsh braking may cause a skid.*

(7) *Don't rest your foot on the clutch pedal.*

(8) *Low gears give most power but little speed. High gears give less power but more speed.*

Getting ready to move

(1) *Check your interior mirror.*

(2) *Check your door mirror.*

(3) *Look over your shoulder.*

You are the only person who can make sure that it is safe to move away from the side of the road.

Remember to:

• Check your interior mirror (1).

• Check your door mirror (2).

• Look for a suitable gap in the traffic.

• Look over your shoulder (3) (right if you are parked on the left; left if you are parked on the right). There are blind spots that you cannot see in the mirrors.

• Check the road ahead (4).

• Check the mirrors again (5).

Now decide:

• Is it safe to move away?

• Do I need to signal? You should signal if there is a vehicle or pedestrian nearby who might need to know you are about to drive away (6).

If you decide it isn't safe to pull away, keep looking, and re-checking your blind spot, until there is a safe gap, before you pull into the road (7).

(4) *Check the road ahead.*

(5) *Check the mirrors again.*

(6) *Give a signal.*

(7) *Re-check your blind spot.*

Moving off under control

(1) *Don't let the car roll backwards.*

(2) *Pull away without jerking.*

Once it is safe to pull away, you must be able to keep the car under control. You must select the appropriate gear and co-ordinate the controls to keep the car stationary while you see if it is safe to move.

If you are on a level road:

• Put the car in first gear.

• Press your foot gently on the accelerator pedal.

• Let the clutch out slowly to the biting point.

• Release the handbrake and let the car creep forwards.

• Let the clutch up smoothly all the way.

If you are facing uphill:

• Put the car in first gear.

• Press the accelerator pedal a bit harder than you would on a level surface. The engine has more work to do, so it needs more power.

• Keep the car stationary or let it move forwards slightly. Do NOT let it roll backwards (1).

• Let the clutch out slowly to the biting point and release the handbrake. Do NOT jerk forwards (2) or allow the car to stall (3). Keep pressing on the gas pedal as you let the clutch out smoothly all the way. Do NOT race the engine (4).

(3) *Don't stall the engine.*

(4) *Don't race the engine.*

17

If you are facing downhill:

• Apply the footbrake.

• Put the car in first gear. (If the hill is very steep (5) use a higher gear.)

• Release the handbrake gently.

• Release the footbrake slowly. As the car starts to roll forwards (6), release the clutch smoothly and fully and press the accelerator gently.

Moving away at an angle

If another car is parked close to your car, you may have to move off at a sharp angle. This procedure is similar to pulling away in a straight line, but remember:

• Use the clutch to keep the car creeping forwards slowly or to hold it still if necessary.

• Turn the steering wheel much more, first to the right, then to the left.

• Be very observant and extra careful (7). Look behind several times as you move away to make sure it is still safe.

• Check the road ahead more carefully. If the road is narrow, you may block the path of any oncoming traffic (8).

You will be asked to carry out this exercise on your driving test!

(5) *Use a higher gear on a very steep hill.*

(6) *The car will roll forwards as you release the footbrake.*

(7) *Be extra careful.*

(8) *Don't block oncoming traffic.*

Emergency stop

If you look very carefully and anticipate all the hazards on the road ahead, you should NEVER have to stop in an emergency. But the unexpected can happen. Most likely, you may have failed to see a danger far enough ahead and may not have reduced your speed in good time.

For this reason, the driving test includes an exercise which is a simulation of a real emergency. The examiner will, usually near the beginning of the test, stop you at the side of the road, and explain that he will shortly want you to carry out an emergency stop. He will demonstrate the signal he will give to tell you when to stop. He will probably explain that he wants you to imagine that a child has run out into the road

(1) *Don't lock the wheels.*

(2) *Grip the steering wheel firmly.*

in front of you. Your main aim should be to stop in the shortest possible distance, without losing control of your car.

Brake progressively. Push the brake pedal down firmly, but not fiercely. Push down harder as the car slows down. Do not brake so hard that you lock the wheels (1). A skidding car is out of control, takes longer to stop and may slide sideways.

Control the steering by tightening your grip on the steering wheel (2). Do not take your hands off the wheel until the car has stopped.

Do not push down the clutch until just before you stop (3). Early use of the clutch stops the engine from assisting the braking and increases the risk of skidding.

Do not put the handbrake on until you have stopped (4).

Do not signal (5). Both hands are needed on the wheel.

Do not check your mirrors before braking (6). You should already know what is behind you.

When you have stopped, make the car safe by putting the handbrake on and selecting neutral. You are likely to have stopped in the middle of the road. Check mirrors and blind spots on BOTH sides of the car before pulling away.

(3) *Brake first and push the clutch down just before stopping.*

(4) *Put the handbrake on only after you have stopped.*

(5) *Don't signal.*

(6) *Don't check the mirrors.*

Reversing

(1) ` Look out for pedestrians, especially children.

(2) The front of your car swings out as you turn the wheel.

(3) Keep looking all around.

The driving test changed slightly on 1 April 1991. From that date the examiner has been able to choose two out of three exercises, involving reverse movements, on which to test you. They are reversing round a corner, turning the car in the road and reverse parking parallel to the kerb. Pages 20-25 explain what is required.

Many learner drivers are a little afraid of reversing. They have heard stories that this is a hard skill to master, and because they believe it is difficult, they often find it so. In reality, reversing a car is not difficult, but going backwards can make steering feel different because the front wheels, which make the car turn, are now at the 'wrong end' of the car.

Looking backwards can seem strange and may cause you to turn the steering wheel in the wrong direction. It is a good idea to practise reversing in a straight line, before you attempt to reverse around a corner. You will find that only tiny movements of the steering wheel are necessary in order to keep the car straight. Try to focus on an object a long way down the road behind the car as this helps you to judge whether you are travelling in a straight line. Remember that if you are on the left side of the road, and you steer to the left, the back of your car will turn in towards the kerb. If you steer to the right, the back of your car will turn away from the kerb.

Reversing can be dangerous, because other drivers and pedestrians do not necessarily expect you to be doing it. For example, a pedestrian may step into the road behind your car, because even if he sees you at the wheel, he will expect you to move off forwards. So you must take care and keep looking. You must not cause inconvenience or danger to other drivers or pedestrians.

On your test, the examiner will ask you to stop by the side of the road just before a side road or opening. He will ask you to drive past the junction, then reverse into it, and to keep reversing back for a reasonable distance. This, in practice, means about three to four car lengths. You should:

• Drive past the turning.

• Look into the turning for any problems as you drive past.

• Stop in a position from which you can reverse safely into it.

Stop about 60 centimetres (2 feet) away from the kerb and at least a car length beyond the corner. Make sure you are parallel to the kerb and that you have stopped with your wheels straight. You will need to turn slightly in your seat, so that you can see to the rear. Look through the back window. Never reverse simply by looking in your mirrors. Look all around before you start to reverse. When you reverse, you must keep the car under full control, keep reasonably close to the kerb and look out for other traffic and pedestrians. Look out particularly for children (1), who may be hidden behind the car. If necessary, get out and look.

Remember, as you turn the wheel, the front end of your car will swing out into the road (2). Look forwards and all around, just before you turn the wheel.

Keep looking all around, the whole of the time you are moving backwards (3). Use clutch control to reverse at a safe speed.

Never reverse from a side road into a major road (4). Do not reverse further than necessary. You may remove your seat belt when reversing. Remember to put it back on again before you drive off. The diagram (5) explains the technique used for reversing to the left.

When you prepare for this exercise, remember to practise reversing around as many different types of corner as possible: right angles and long curves, and both up and down on hills.

(4) *Never reverse from a side road into a main road.*

(5) *Reversing to the left. The examiner asks you to stop just before the corner* (A). *Position your car about 60 centimetres from the kerb* (B). *Look all around before turning the wheel* (C). *Keep reasonably close to the kerb* (D). *Continue to reverse back for three to four car lengths* (E).

Turning in the road

(1) *Check your blind spot before moving.*

(2) *Turn the car in as few moves as possible.*

(3) *Do not let the wheels touch the kerb.*

Every driver will need to turn around in the road at some time or other. If there are no side roads or openings you can reverse into, and the road is not wide enough to allow you to make a U-turn, you will need to turn your car around by a series of forward and backward movements. This is often, but incorrectly, called a three-point turn. The number of movements needed to complete the turn will depend on the width of the road, the length of your car, its steering lock and your ability to handle the controls.

On your driving test, the examiner will ask you to pull up on the left at a convenient place. He will expect you to complete the exercise in as few moves as possible, without touching the kerbs. You must show you are in full control of the car, and be careful not to cause any danger to other traffic or pedestrians.

Make sure you have stopped in a suitable place. Move along the road a little if necessary before you start.

Look out for pedestrians. They can be alarmed by a car turning across the road towards them.

Look out for other traffic. You will be partly blocking the road. Give way if necessary.

Check your blind spot before moving (1).

(4) *Turn the steering wheel only when the car is moving.*

Turn the car in as few moves as possible (2).

Do not let the wheels touch the kerb (3).

Turn the steering wheel only when the car is moving (4).

You may remove your seat belt to complete this exercise.

The diagram opposite (5) illustrates how to turn in the road safely and efficiently.

(5) *Turning in the road.*
Use clutch control to creep slowly forwards (A), turning the wheel quickly and fully to the right. Keep looking all around (B).

When the front of the car is about a metre from the kerb, steer quickly to the left, braking to a stop before the front wheels touch the kerb (C). Look at the camber of the road. The curve in the road surface may cause the car to speed up.

Put the handbrake on, and prepare to reverse. Use clutch control to hold the car still, and look all around before moving backwards.

Use clutch control to creep slowly backwards (D), steering quickly to the left. Keep looking all around, particularly over your right shoulder. The right side of the car will reach the kerb first.

When the back of the car is about a metre from the kerb, steer quickly to the right. Brake to a stop just before the boot of the car overhangs the kerb, *and before the rear wheels touch the kerb (E).*

Put the handbrake on and prepare to move the car forwards. Look all around before moving. Drive slowly forwards, steering as necessary to reach the left-hand side of the road (F).

Park on the left, and put your seat belt back on.

Reverse parking

Finding somewhere safe and suitable to park is never easy, especially in town. Reversing into a parking space allows you to make use of smaller gaps.

In fact, in today's traffic conditions it has become essential that every driver can perform this task safely and efficiently, and without holding up other traffic for longer than absolutely necessary. For this reason, since 1 April 1991, reverse parking has been added to the exercises that can be set on your driving test. You may now be asked to complete this exercise instead of turning your car in the road or reversing round a corner.

Parking in a car park
Most car parks are marked out in bays, which clearly show you where you are allowed to park.

(1) Reverse into the gap.

As many car parks operate a one-way system, you are also likely to see arrows and signs showing you where to go. Not only are car parks very busy places, but the spaces inside them can often be quite small. When you have found an empty bay, it is usually simplest and safest to reverse into it (1). Your car is more manoeuvrable in reverse gear, which makes it easier to fit into the available gap. Look all around your car for any

dangers before moving backwards. When you are ready to leave, you can drive out forwards. This makes it much easier to see other vehicles and pedestrians.

Reverse parking between two vehicles
You need a minimum gap of about one and a half times the length of your car (2).

Drive slightly past the gap and stop parallel to the front parked car and about one metre away from it (3). Look carefully all around. Remember that the front of your car will swing out as you turn the wheel.

Reverse slowly with a slight left lock, and watch the rear corner of the front parked car. Straighten the wheels and

(2) You need a gap about one and a half times the length of your car.

(3) Stop parallel to the front parked car and about one metre away from it.

(4) Reverse slowly with a slight left lock. Remember that the front of the car will swing out as you move.

(5) As you clear the parked car in front, steer slightly, and then fully, to the right.

(6) As the front of your car nears the kerb, straighten the wheels.

(7) If necessary, move backwards or forwards to straighten up.

(8) *For your first few attempts, select a very quiet road.*

Remember, too, that car owners can become very nervous if they see you getting too close to the vehicle which is their pride and joy. So, to start with, choose a gap of at least two to three car lengths in order to allow a safety margin for error. As your skills improve, you can gradually select smaller gaps

Your driving test

If the examiner requires you to complete the reverse parking exercise as part of your driving test, he will point out a parked car and ask you to reverse park behind it. He will expect you to be able to park safely at the kerb by reversing into the space of about two car lengths.

It is important to understand that on many occasions there will not be a car parked at the rear of the space into which you are going to reverse.

You should signal if necessary, drive alongside the car pointed out by the examiner, and position your car so that you can complete the exercise safely and correctly.

You should then look carefully all around and reverse behind the parked car. If there is no car to the rear of the space, you will need to use your imagination and pretend that one is there. You should make a point of practising this before you take your test and, in particular, ensure that you can judge your

(9) *When practising, take care not to annoy local residents.*

distance from the kerb without the help of a parked car behind on which to focus. You should, of course, finish the exercise stopped parallel and reasonably close to the kerb.

continue to reverse into the gap (4). As you clear the front parked car, steer slightly to the right, and then fully to the right (5).

Look at the nearside headlamp of the rear parked car to help you judge your position. As the front of your car nears the kerb, straighten the wheels (6). If necessary, move backwards or forwards to straighten up. Finish in the middle of the gap (7).

The British School of Motoring strongly recommends that you only practise this exercise with an Approved Driving Instructor, and in a car with dual controls.

For your first few attempts, you should select a very quiet road where you will cause least inconvenience to other traffic (8). It is important that you warn any other drivers of your intention by giving an early signal when necessary.

When practising, take care not to annoy local residents (9).

Do:

• Signal early if necessary.

• Look all around for traffic and pedestrians before you reverse and keep looking until you have completed the manoeuvre.

• Use clutch control to keep a slow and steady speed.

Don't:

• Get too close to the parked cars.

• Mount the kerb.

• Cause danger to others.

• Park too far away from the kerb.

Using the mirrors

(1) *A driver may be close behind.*

Whenever you are driving, you need to know as much about what is happening on the road behind you as you do about what is taking place in front. The situation behind can change very quickly. This means that you must look in your mirrors frequently and always be aware of what may be in your blind spots.

Just looking is not enough. You must also act sensibly and safely on what you see. That is what the examiner is looking for when you take your driving test. He is trained to spot your eye movements, but he will pay most attention to whether your actions after you look are safe and sensible. For example, if you move out around a parked car when another driver is overtaking you, it makes little difference how many times you move your eyes towards your mirrors. You should not move out until the overtaking vehicle has passed you.

You must always use your mirrors before doing anything which might affect other road users, such as:

• Signalling.

• Changing direction.

• Turning left or right.

• Overtaking or changing lanes.

• Stopping or slowing down.

• Increasing speed.

• Opening your car door.

What sort of things should you look for, and what action should you take?

A driver may be close behind you (1).

Look well ahead for the need to slow down or stop. Start braking early. Your brake lights give a warning signal to the driver behind, and if you spread your braking over a long distance, you are less likely to be hit from the rear.

A driver may be in an overtaking position coming up behind (2).

Look well ahead for the need to pull out. Give an early signal if you need to, and check again to see how the other driver reacts. See whether he stays back or continues to gain on you. If in doubt, don't pull out.

A bicycle or motorbike rider may come through where there is no room for a car (3).

Be especially careful if you intend to turn left or right. Check your door mirrors as well as your interior mirror. Give a signal and check to see what the rider does. Decide when to turn: before or after the bike reaches you.

A driver may be overtaking on a dual carriageway (4).

(2) *A driver may be in an overtaking position coming up behind.*

(3) *A rider may come through where there is no room for a car.*

(4) *There may be a driver overtaking on a dual carriageway.*

other way lies hesitancy and the taking of risks.

Watch out for cars and pedestrians close by when you park (5). Look before you open your car doors and wait if necessary until it is safe.

Many learner drivers make the mistake of thinking that frequent use of the mirrors is unnecessary except to satisfy the examiner on their driving test. Some people on test even set the angle of the mirror so that they have to move their head to see in it. They believe that this will impress the examiner favourably, whereas it is, of course, likely to do just the opposite. When you have passed your driving test, remember that you cannot make sensible decisions without information. To get the information, you must look, and that includes looking in your mirrors.

Look for parked cars ahead. You will have to change to the right-hand lane to get past. You need to ask yourself: Is it safe to move out? No, because a car is overtaking. Will it be safe after that? Yes. Do I need to signal? Yes, because otherwise the next car behind may also try to overtake me.

If you have been using your mirrors regularly, you will already know the answers to these questions. A quick check before you act, to confirm them, is all you need. If you haven't been using your mirrors, you will not have enough time to make sufficient checks to be certain of any of the answers.

It is easier to know what is happening all the time and just to confirm it when a problem arises than to wait for the problem to arise and try to get all the information you need quickly. One way lies confidence, and the

(5) *Look for cars and pedestrians close by when you park.*

Giving signals

Signals are the language of driving. They warn other road users that we are there, or that we intend to change speed or direction in some way.

To be of any use, it is important that:

• Everyone understands what they mean. For this reason you should only give the signals shown in the Highway Code.

(1) *A right signal?*

(2) *A left signal?*

• They are given early and clearly enough for others to see them and respond to them.

• They are not misleading or confusing.

Signals can be given in a variety of ways: direction indicators; arm signals; brake lights; horn; headlights; reversing lights.

On your driving test, your examiner will expect you to signal in plenty of time whenever it would help another road user. In busy towns, you will nearly always need to give a signal when turning left or right. But there is no point in giving a signal if there is no one who could benefit from it. For example, if you are moving off from the side of the road and the street is deserted, you should not signal. This will also help show the examiner that you are thinking about what you do.

Always check your mirrors before you signal. Remember that when you signal, you are communicating your intentions, not giving instructions, to other road users. The signal does not give you a right to do anything unless it is safe to do it. You can only know this if you look first.

Direction indicators
Direction indicators are the normal way of informing others that you intend to change direction. Make sure the signal is cancelled after you have completed the manoeuvre.

A right signal (1) means either that you intend to move out to the right, or turn right.

A left signal (2) means you intend to move in to the left, or stop on the left, or turn left.

Do not give confusing signals (3). For example, if you signal right to pull out round a parked car, make sure that this will not be mistaken for a signal to turn into a junction on your right.

Do not signal too early (4). If there are two side roads close together, a signal given too soon may make people think you are going to turn before you actually do.

Time your signal carefully if you intend to stop on the left (5). If you are stopping just beyond a junction, do not signal until you pass it. Otherwise, a driver waiting to emerge may think you are turning left and pull out in front of you.

Do not signal too late (6). A driver who suddenly decides that the junction on the right is the road he wishes to take and brakes, signals right and cuts across oncoming traffic, is causing danger.

Arm signals
For most occasions when you intend to change direction, an indicator is better than an arm signal because:

- It can be seen more easily, especially at night.

- It can be given for longer.

- It allows you to keep both hands on the steering wheel.

But your indicators may fail to work one day, so you should make sure you can give the arm signals shown in the Highway Code.

Never wave pedestrians across the road (7). You could put them in danger from another vehicle.

Brake lights
Early and progressive braking gives drivers behind you time to see your brake lights and warns them that you are slowing down.

Horn
Use your horn to warn of your presence.

Never use your horn as a rebuke.

Never use your horn when close to animals.

Headlights
Flashing your headlights has the same meaning as sounding your horn. It lets other people know you are there. When another driver flashes his headlights, you must treat this signal as a warning, and not as an invitation to proceed.

Reversing lights
When you select reverse gear, white lights at the back of most cars indicate to other road users that you intend to reverse.

(5) *Time signals carefully.*

(3) *Do not give confusing signals.*

(6) *Do not signal too late.*

(4) *Do not signal too early.*

(7) *Never beckon people across the road.*

Acting on signs and signals

(1) *No entry ahead: you will have to turn right.*

(2) *You may go on if it is safe and clear.*

(3) *Signals may not be working.*

Everywhere you drive, you will see road signs, and markings painted on the road. They are there to help you, and they can only do that if you understand what they all mean. As a general rule, the more paint that there is on the road, the more dangers you are likely to encounter. For example, on a straight stretch of road, there will often be short white lines with long gaps between them painted in the centre. As the road nears a bend or junction, the white lines get longer and the gaps are reduced. These are hazard warning lines, and advise you of a potential danger ahead. A safe driver will reduce speed and take extra care when he sees these hazard lines.

You must act correctly at traffic light signals, and obey signals given by police officers, traffic wardens and school crossing patrols. All these signals are given to help you, and to keep the traffic flowing as smoothly as possible. You can cause chaos or danger if you ignore them.

On your driving test, the examiner will expect you to follow the road ahead unless he asks you to turn, and unless the road signs or markings tell you to do otherwise. Here are some examples of the signs and signals you will meet.

The road ahead is marked with red signs with white horizontal bars (1). This is the 'no entry' sign. The examiner will not tell you this. You are expected to 'read the road' yourself.

(4) *Box junction: do not enter unless your exit is clear.*

(5) *Driver ahead signals right.*

You will almost certainly go through a set of traffic signals (2). The examiner will expect to see you check that it is safe and clear to drive through, even though the light is showing green.

If the lights are not working, you may see the sign illustrated (3). You will need to take special care. Approach the junction slowly and be ready to give way to traffic.

STOP

Vehicle approaching from the front

Vehicles approaching from both front and behind

Vehicle approaching from behind

COME ON

Beckoning a vehicle on from the front

Beckoning a vehicle on from the side

Beckoning a vehicle on from behind

(6) *Signals given by traffic controllers.*

In the middle of a junction you may see a yellow box grid road marking (4). You must not enter the yellow box unless your exit is clear. However, you can wait in the box when turning right, as long as it is only the oncoming traffic that prevents you from completing the turn. Your exit must still be clear. Your examiner will expect you to spot road markings like this, and act correctly.

Be aware of the signals that other road users give and act on them sensibly.

If the driver ahead has to wait before turning right (5), and there is room to overtake on the left, the examiner will expect you to 'read' this situation early and go past on the left.

Sometimes there may be police or traffic wardens controlling the traffic. You will need to know what their signals mean, so that you can comply with them (6).

Care in the use of speed

Modern cars are capable of being driven safely at high speeds, especially on roads designed for this purpose. The average speed of traffic on

(1) *Keep to the speed limits.*

motorways is, for example, much higher than that of traffic on busy main roads in town. Despite the terrible accidents that occur on motorways, they are, nevertheless, statistically the safest of all our roads. So driving fast is not in itself what causes accidents. But driving too fast in the wrong place at the wrong time can be highly dangerous. At 10.30 in the morning, it may be safe to drive along a certain road at 30mph. The same road at 3.30 in the afternoon, when the schools are emptying out, is a very different place. Driving at 30mph now might well be too fast for the conditions. The same road in the wet would mean that you need to reduce speed further. It

(2) *30mph = 14 metres (45 feet) per second.*

takes longer to stop when it is wet – up to twice the normal distance – and the risk of skidding is greatly increased. In icy conditions, it may take you as much as ten times the distance to stop as when the road is dry. In circumstances like these, it

(3) *Know your stopping distances.*

(4) *Restricted vision means less speed.*

What is meant by 'a safe speed'?

You must of course obey the speed limits (1). Speed limits state the maximum speed at which you are allowed to drive. They do not mean that it is safe to drive at that speed.

Never drive so fast that you cannot stop well within the distance you can see to be clear. At 30mph your car will be travelling about 14 metres (45 feet) every second (2). That's a very long way.

Know your stopping distances (3).

Slow down whenever your view of the road ahead is restricted (4): before bends or on the brow of a hill, or in bad weather.

Slow down whenever your space is restricted (5). Less space equals less speed, whether you are in narrow roads, or in roads narrowed by parked cars, road works or other obstructions.

Slow down when you are forced to drive close to parked cars (6). A door may open. A car may pull off. A child might run out.

Leave enough space between you and the vehicle in front so that you can brake safely if it slows down or stops suddenly (7).

On an open road in good weather, leave a gap of one metre for each mile per hour of your speed, or a two-second time gap may be enough (8).

(6) *Parked cars may pull off or a child may run out.*

(5) *Less space = less speed.*

does not matter whether or not you are slightly more alert or have faster reactions than another driver. If you are driving too fast, you will have little chance of stopping, however good you are. Common sense suggests that your only way to stay safe is to slow down.

On your driving test the examiner will want to see that you do not drive too fast for the road and traffic conditions. He will also be looking to see if you keep a safe distance between yourself and the vehicle in front.

(7) *Keep enough space between you and the car in front.*

(8) *Leave a two-second gap.*

Making progress

(1) *A clear road. You should drive at the speed limit or just below it.*

In the last section, we talked about the need to take care and to drive at a safe speed. What is often not realised is that being too hesitant or driving too slowly can be just as dangerous as driving too fast.

Our roads are very busy and overcrowded, and the pace of life in the 1990s makes most people think that they have to be in a hurry. The vast majority of drivers want to arrive at their destination as quickly as is safely possible. Their progress will often be frustrated by the sheer volume of traffic. Most drivers make allowance for this. They expect some traffic jams and hold-ups and set out on their journey with enough time to compensate for the problems. But when they see a clear stretch of road, they want to get moving and make up for lost time. There is nothing more frustrating than getting stuck for miles behind a driver who appears to be sightseeing; a driver who crawls along at a speed far below the speed limit or a safe speed for the road conditions. Tempers start to fray and judgement becomes impaired. This can cause people to try to overtake when it is not safe to do so. Frustration can easily lead to accidents.

A similar frustration is often caused at junctions, where the driver ahead seems to have fallen asleep, and does not take advantage of gaps in the traffic. The inexperienced driver tends to wait for a gap and then get ready

(3) *Look out for speed limit signs.*

(2) *Don't crawl along too slowly when it is not necessary, as you may hold up other traffic.*

(4) *Don't stop when the way is clear.*

to go. By the time he is ready, the gap may have disappeared. A more experienced driver will try to anticipate the gap. He will put a lot of energy into looking and asking himself continuously whether he could go after the next car. If he thinks this is possible, he will get ready, make his decision and go if it is safe to do so. Because he is ready and has made his decision earlier, he will need a far smaller gap in order to progress safely.

On your driving test, your examiner will want to see you make reasonable progress. Oddly enough, more people fail the driving test for lack of progress than for driving too fast. Too much caution betrays a lack of confidence, which may cause the examiner to question the driver's ability.

On a clear road you should drive at the speed limit or just below it. This helps keep the traffic flowing smoothly (1). Don't crawl along too slowly when it is not necessary (2). You may hold up other traffic. The examiner will regard this as a fault. Look out for speed limit signs and act on them (3). For example, if you are driving along a road and you see a 40mph speed limit sign, increase your speed well above 30mph if it is safe to do so. In this way, you will show the examiner that you have noticed the road sign, and that you have judged that a higher speed is safe and appropriate.

Don't stop when the way is clear for you to proceed. If you are turning right, and you can see that there is no oncoming traffic, there is no need to stop (4).

Don't stop at 'give way' lines if the way ahead is clear (5). Slow down and start to look as you approach the 'give way' lines. If you can see that the way ahead is clear, keep moving. If you cannot see well into the new road, slow down even more and stop if necessary.

Don't hesitate unnecessarily when emerging at junctions (6). Stay alert, keep looking and try to anticipate a safe gap in the traffic. Always be ready to move away at the FIRST safe opportunity.

(5) *Don't stop at 'give way' lines if the way is clear.*

Do:

• Drive at the speed limit, or just below it, when safe to do so.

Don't:

• Crawl along when it is not necessary.

• Stop at 'give way' lines if the way ahead is clear.

• Hesitate unnecessarily at junctions.

(6) *Don't hesitate unnecessarily when emerging at junctions. Stay alert and be ready to move away at the FIRST safe opportunity.*

Road junctions and roundabouts

(1) *A 'stop' sign.*

(2) *A 'give way' sign.*

(3) *Unmarked junctions.*

Statistics show that more accidents occur at or near junctions than at any other place on the road. Most of these accidents are caused by human error. The inability to deal with junctions safely is a frequent reason why learner drivers fail the driving test.

Priority

Because traffic meets at junctions, it is necessary to have rules which allow everyone to proceed safely, and which help maintain the best possible traffic flow.

To achieve this, traffic from a particular direction is given priority, that is, allowed to proceed first if it is safe to do so. At many busy junctions, traffic lights change the priority from one direction to another. At other junctions, the vehicles on one road always have priority over the vehicles on another. Road signs and markings are provided to tell you who has priority:

- At a 'stop' sign you do not have priority (1). You must stop and give way until it is safe for you to proceed.

- At a 'give way' sign you do not have priority (2). You must give way and you must stop when necessary in order to give priority to other drivers.

- At unmarked junctions (3) there are no road signs or markings, and all vehicles have equal priority. Take great care.

(4) *Even where you have priority, be prepared for the driver who may pull out in front of you.*

Approaching junctions safely

When you are driving along a main road, you must still take account of all the side roads as you approach them.

Even where you have priority, be prepared for the driver who may pull out in front of you (4).

On approach to any junction you must always:

- Check your mirrors.

- Signal your intentions if necessary.

- Take up the correct position as early as possible.

- Adjust your speed, and be ready to stop if necessary.

- Look. You should look particularly for:
  Road signs and markings.
  Pedestrians who may be about to cross the road.
  Other traffic.

(5) *A clear junction. Imagine that you wish to turn left. Nothing is blocking your vision and you can see a long way in both directions into the new road. Check your mirrors and signal your intention to turn (A). Keep well to the left (B). Reduce speed enough to allow time to assess the junction (C). You see 'give way' lines and start to look left and right. You can see very early that it is safe to proceed (D). You are unlikely to have to stop, so continue to reduce speed and select a suitable gear to make the turn (E). Keep looking all around (F). Make a final check all around before entering the main road (G).*

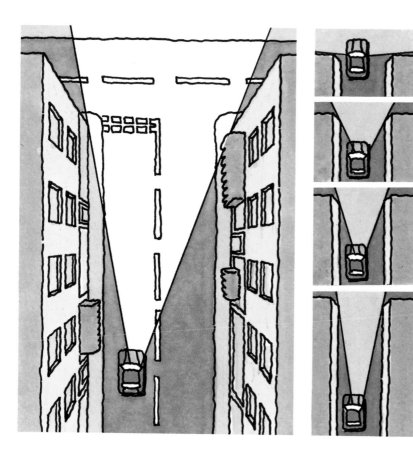

(6) *A junction where sight lines are blocked by buildings. As you approach this junction, it becomes obvious that you will have to stop. You cannot see clearly until you reach the end of the road, and your front wheels are about to cross the 'give way' lines. If you are still moving at this point, you will be half way out into the main road before you are sure it is safe.*

(7) A junction where sight lines are blocked by buildings and parked cars. This junction is the same type as that illustrated in the previous diagram but, here, the added problem of parked cars in the main road restricts your vision even further. Imagine that there are 'give way' lines for pedestrians (A) and be prepared to stop if necessary. You must stop at the end of the road (B) but you still cannot see properly to the right and left around the parked cars. Edge forward under clutch control to where you again imagine a set of 'give way' lines and stop again if necessary (C). Keep looking to the right and left and drive on when it is safe.

(8) Give way to traffic on the roundabout approaching from your immediate right.

Pulling out of a side road safely

The way to pull out of a side road safely depends on what you can see, and how soon you can see it. It is helpful to think of three general types of junction:

• A clear junction (5) (see previous page).

• A junction where sight lines are blocked by buildings (6) (see previous page).

• A junction where sight lines are blocked by buildings and parked cars (7).

The illustrations and captions explain the correct procedures.

Roundabouts

Roundabouts are designed to help keep everyone moving by mixing together several streams of traffic.

Give way to traffic on the roundabout approaching from your immediate right (8).

Do not stop if it is safe to keep moving (9). Signal and position your car correctly for the exit you wish to take.

If you are taking the first exit on the left (10):

• Approach in the left-hand lane.

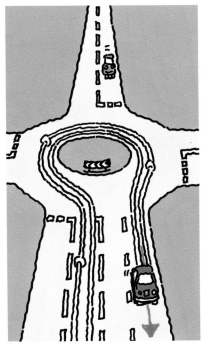

(9) *Do not stop if it is safe to keep moving.*

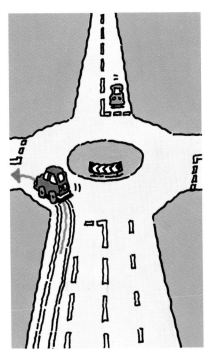

(10) *Taking the first exit on the left.*

• Signal left.

• Keep to the left.

If you are going straight ahead (11):

• Approach in the left-hand lane.

• Do not signal on approach.

• Keep in the left-hand lane.

• Signal left here (A).

If you are taking an exit to the right (12):

• Signal right.

• Approach in the right-hand lane.

• Keep to the right and continue to signal right.

• Here (A), cancel signal, check mirrors and left blind spot, signal left.

• Leave by the left-hand lane of the exit road unless it is blocked.

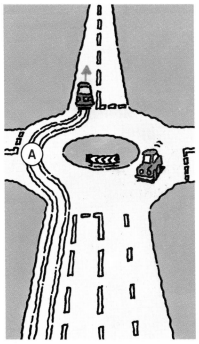

(11) *Going straight ahead.*

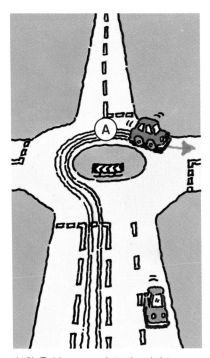

(12) *Taking an exit to the right.*

Overtaking, meeting and crossing the path of other vehicles

Overtaking

(1) *The road markings forbid certain actions.*

Overtaking another moving vehicle is potentially the most dangerous driving situation, particularly on single carriageway roads, where oncoming traffic will be meeting you head on. A large number of accidents are caused by drivers who overtake in the wrong place or at the wrong time. Inexperienced drivers are frequently overtaken while they are learning to drive. They need to practise the skills of overtaking safely before driving alone.

(4) *You might cause danger to other road users.*

On your driving test you may well catch up with slow-moving traffic. Milk floats and cyclists, for example, will be travelling slower than you. The examiner will expect you to overtake any slow-moving traffic when it is safe to do so.

Do not overtake where:

(2) *The road signs forbid certain actions.*

• Road markings forbid you (1).

• Road signs forbid you (2).

• You cannot see far enough ahead (3) at or near:
    A corner or bend.
    A hump-backed bridge.
    The brow of a hill.

You might cause danger to other road users:

(3) *You cannot see far enough ahead.*

• At or near a road junction (4).

• At a level crossing.

• Where the road narrows.

(5) *How far ahead can you see clearly?*

(6) *The speed of the vehicle to be overtaken and the speed and performance of your own car are vital.*

• At any type of pedestrian crossing.

Deciding to overtake

You need to think about:

• How far ahead you can see clearly (5).

• The speed of the vehicle to be overtaken. The time you will take to pass another vehicle will depend on the difference between the speeds at which the cars are travelling and the speed and performance of your own car (6).

• The speed and distance away of approaching vehicles (7). Two vehicles coming towards each other at 55mph will be closing the gap between them at 110mph. That is about 50 metres (165 feet) every second.

• The road surface and weather conditions, like fog (8).

• The distance, speed and position of following vehicles (9).

Overtaking a cyclist

Look well ahead and try to spot any cyclist early. Check behind.

Is it safe to overtake? If someone is overtaking you, or if overtaking will cause problems with oncoming traffic, then the answer is 'NO' (10).

When can you overtake? If you cannot go straight past (11), you will need to slow down in order to follow at a safe distance.

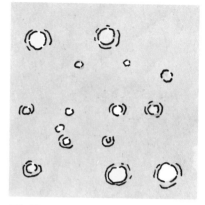

(8) *The road surface and weather conditions like fog play a crucial role.*

(7) *Assess the speed and distance away of approaching vehicles.*

(9) *Check the distance, speed and position of following vehicles.*

(10) *Is it safe to overtake?*

(11) *When can you overtake?*

(12) *Do you need to signal?*

Do you need to signal? When you do see a safe time to overtake, a signal will help any traffic ahead or behind you (12).

Give cyclists plenty of room (13). They may wobble or swerve suddenly. Go well past before moving back to the left.

Remember: If in doubt, don't overtake.

Meeting other traffic

Meeting oncoming traffic simply means going past vehicles that are travelling in the opposite direction. You will frequently come across situations where the road ahead is too narrow for two vehicles to pass each other safely, particularly when driving in towns.

Look well ahead for reasons why the road may get narrower, like parked cars (14).

Look for warning road signs (15) and try to time your arrival at the point where the road narrows so that you do not have to stop. Slowing down early may mean the oncoming traffic has passed through before you get there.

Look well ahead for gaps in the parked cars where you can pull in and give way if necessary (16).

Sometimes you will have to squeeze through a very narrow space (17). Go very slowly so that you have time to judge the gap.

(13) *Give the cyclist plenty of room and go well past before moving back to the left.*

(14) *Look well ahead for parked cars.*

(15) *Look for warning road signs and try to time your arrival at the point where the road narrows, so that you do not have to stop.*

Crossing the path of other traffic

When you turn right, you usually have to cross the path of other traffic. You must learn to judge how much time you need in order to make your turn safely. If you are able to anticipate a gap in the oncoming traffic, you may be able to slow down and complete your turn without ever having to stop. If your car is still moving, you will be able to make safe use of smaller gaps in the oncoming traffic. Once your car is stopped, you need extra time to get it moving again. Oncoming vehicles should not have to stop, slow down or swerve to allow you to complete the turn. If the road is busy, you will often have to stop and wait for a safe gap. If this is the case, make sure you position your car correctly. This position is normally just to the left of the centre of the road.

Look for gaps in the oncoming traffic (18). Without inconveniencing other road users, try to time your arrival at the junction so that you do not have to stop. Slowing down sooner often means you can arrive when there is a gap in the traffic.

In judging a safe gap, look at the approaching traffic and ask yourself whether you would walk across the road in front of that car (19). If the answer is 'yes', make your turn. If the answer is 'no', or 'I don't know', don't go.

(17) *Sometimes you will have to squeeze through a very narrow space. Go very slowly to enable you to judge the gap.*

(18) *Look for gaps in the oncoming traffic.*

(16) *Look well ahead for gaps in the parked cars where you can pull in and give way if necessary.*

(19) *Judging a safe gap.*

Position on the road

(1) *Don't drive too close to the centre of the road.*

(2) *Don't drive too close to the kerb.*

(3) *Traffic ahead may turn right.*

(4) *Return to the left after passing obstructions in the road.*

The basic rule is keep to the left except when overtaking or turning right.

Don't drive too close to the centre of the road (1). This reduces the safety gap between you and oncoming traffic.

Don't drive too close to the kerb (2). The bumps and drains in the gutter make steering control difficult. More importantly, you will be too close to pedestrians and have less time to react if they step into the road.

Traffic ahead may turn right (3). Be ready to go through on the left if there is room.

Return to the left after passing obstructions in the road (4).

Do not weave in and out of frequent obstructions. Maintain a steady course (5).

Drive in the middle of your lane (6).

Select the lane for the direction you intend to take (7).

Watch out for filter lanes at traffic lights (8).

(5) *Do not weave in and out of frequent obstructions. Maintain a steady course.*

(6) *Drive in the middle of your lane.*

(7) *Select the lane for the direction you intend to take.*

(8) *Watch out for filter lanes at traffic lights.*

Passing stationary vehicles

(1) *Allow plenty of room.*

When you are driving around town, there are very few roads where you will not have to pass stationary vehicles. Cars will be parked in most side roads; even on main roads, delivery vehicles and buses will be stopped at the side of the road. You must allow plenty of room when passing stationary vehicles. Look out for dangers and be prepared to slow down.

Where possible, allow at least a car door's width between you and the parked cars (1). If you can't do this, slow down.

Don't drive too close. What if someone opens the door (2)? Look for people sitting in the driver's seat.

What if the stationary vehicle moves off (3)? Be ready to stop.

What if a child runs out into the road (4)? Look for feet under the cars, and be ready to stop.

Watch out for a cyclist who may pull out round the parked car without stopping (5).

Watch out for people coming out in front of a bus at a bus stop (6).

(2) *Don't drive too close. What if someone opens the door?*

(3) *What if the car moves off? Be ready to stop.*

(4) *What if a child runs out into the road?*

(5) *Watch out for cyclists.*

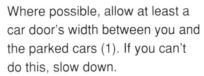

(6) *Watch out for people coming out in front of a bus at a bus stop.*

Pedestrian crossings

(1) *Look well ahead for zebra crossings. You may be able simply to slow down and time your arrival for when the crossing is clear.*

(2) *Check your mirrors and slow down early.*

(3) *Look for pedestrians on the pavements who may reach the crossing before you, and be prepared to give way.*

The volume of traffic on today's roads means that pedestrians often have considerable difficulty crossing anything but a quiet side road in safety. Drivers are often in a hurry, but can easily forget that pedestrians are no less pressed for time. Both drivers and pedestrians make mistakes, especially when they are in a rush. The driver is, to a certain extent, protected by his car. A minor accident is likely to damage the vehicle, but not the driver. Pedestrians have no such protection, and the slightest collision with a car can, as the accident statistics demonstrate, cause serious injury.

Pedestrian crossings are provided to help people cross the road safely. We have all been pedestrians, and with few exceptions, even the most experienced driver is still a pedestrian at times. It is a good idea to ask yourself what you expect drivers to do when you wish to use a crossing. You expect them to show consideration, and to slow down or stop to let you cross. You may expect this, but you are unlikely to depend on it happening. You are probably very careful when you try to cross the road on any type of crossing. Most of us realise, after a few near misses, that many drivers simply do not seem to see us, or if they do, seem to ignore our safety.

Before you take your driving test, you may find it useful to act out the part of a pedestrian. Find a

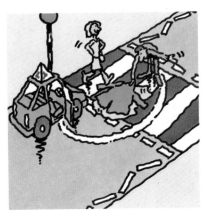

(4) *Be considerate, and give way to people who are waiting to cross.*

(5) *Reduce speed if your vision is restricted.*

(6) *Do not park within the zig-zag lines. It is dangerous and illegal.*

(7) *Do not overtake on approach to a crossing.*

(8) *Do not invite pedestrians to cross. Let them decide for themselves.*

busy crossing and cross the road several times in both directions. Make a note of the drivers who seem to slow down and stop with ease, those who see you far too late, and those who seem not to notice you at all. Then when you drive again, consider the advice that follows, and you should never have trouble giving way in good time.

Zebra crossings

At a zebra crossing, you must by law give way to people on the crossing. Look well ahead for zebra crossings. You can often see the beacons a long way in the distance. You may be able simply to slow down and time your arrival when the crossing is clear (1).

Check your mirrors and slow down early (2). Your brake lights will warn the drivers behind.

Look for pedestrians on the pavements who may reach the crossing before you (3). Be prepared to give way.

Be considerate, and give way to people who are waiting to cross (4).

Reduce your speed if your vision is restricted (5).

Do not park within the white zig-zag lines (6). It is dangerous because it blocks the view of drivers approaching the crossing and makes it more difficult for pedestrians to see oncoming traffic. It is also illegal.

Do not overtake when approaching a crossing (7).

Do not invite pedestrians to cross (8). Let them decide for themselves.

Pelican crossings

Pelican crossings are controlled by traffic lights. The sequence of the lights is green, amber, red, flashing amber, green. Look well ahead and reduce speed early.

(9) *Look for pedestrians who are about to push the button.*

(10) *Be extra careful when the flashing amber light is showing.*

Look for pedestrians who are about to push the button (9). The lights sometimes change very soon after the button is pressed.

Be extra careful when the flashing amber is showing (10). You may drive on, provided that the crossing is clear. People may rush out at the last minute, so always look carefully.

Selecting a safe position for normal stops

(1) *Pull up close to the edge of the road.*

If you live in a busy town, you will have noticed, even as a pedestrian, some of the problems that drivers cause by stopping or parking in dangerous or unsuitable places. In many ways, we are all to blame, and can all be inconsiderate. The man on his way to work who parks on the corner to buy his paper risks causing an accident. The mother who collects her child from school and double parks in order to avoid a walk with the baby creates an equal danger. Every time we park in such thoughtless ways, we place other people's lives at risk.

You should not park or stop even for a few moments in any place where you might cause danger or inconvenience to other road users.

When you are taking your driving test, the examiner will ask you on several occasions to pull up on the left at a convenient place. He may wish to give you the instructions for one of the set exercises, like the emergency stop.

Remember that it sometimes may not be safe to stop immediately. Always check your mirror first, see if there is anyone close behind, and decide if a signal will be necessary.

Pull up close to the edge of the road (1).

(2) *Don't stop where you will make it difficult for others to see clearly.*

(3) *Don't stop where it would make the road too narrow.*

(4) *Don't stop where it would block an entrance.*

Don't stop where you will make it difficult for others to see clearly, such as at or near a road junction (2).

Don't stop where it would make the road narrow, such as opposite another stationary vehicle (3).

Don't stop where it would block an entrance, such as a person's driveway (4).

Don't stop where it could cause danger, especially at or near a school entrance (5).

(5) *Don't stop where it could cause danger, especially at or near a school entrance.*

Awareness and anticipation

(1) *Slow down anywhere near children who are playing and take extra care near schools.*

(2) *Drive slowly past ice cream vans.*

(3) *A ball in the road may be followed by a child.*

Driving a car safely requires your total concentration, something which nearly everyone finds difficult. Most of us can focus all our energy and attention on a difficult task, but we can rarely sustain this level of concentration for more than a few minutes at a time. We are easily distracted. We tire quickly and part of our attention wanders to another problem. Because of this, drivers make mistakes, and so do pedestrians, especially the very young and the elderly. Two out of every three pedestrians killed or seriously injured on the roads are either under 15 or over 60.

The earlier you can spot a possible problem, the easier you will be able to deal with it safely. You can avoid the need for a sudden action, such as harsh braking, that could cause danger to yourself or others.

As soon as you spot a potential problem, you must decide what action you need to take, and then respond as necessary. The faster you are travelling, the less time you have in which to do this. You will often need to reduce your speed simply to give yourself more time to think. As you drive along, you must stay alert, and continually look well ahead and all around for any possible problems that may arise. Every time your vision is restricted or your space is reduced, slow down and give yourself more time to look, and think, and act.

(4) *When turning left or right, give way to pedestrians.*

(5) *Be patient with the elderly and allow them time.*

(6) *Watch out for pedestrians who don't look in the wind or the rain.*

(7) *Give cyclists plenty of room. A cyclist glancing over his right shoulder may turn right in front of you.*

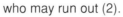

who may run out (2).

A ball in the road may be followed by a child (3).

When turning left or right, give way to pedestrians (4).

Be patient with the elderly and allow them time (5). Sound your horn to warn, but not to rebuke.

Watch out for pedestrians who don't look carefully when it is windy or raining (6).

Give cyclists plenty of room (7). A cyclist who glances over his right shoulder may turn right in front of you.

Watch out for motorbikes and cyclists when turning left (8). Use your nearside door mirror to spot them.

Watch out for the bike that squeezes through the gaps in the traffic (9).

(9) *Look for the bike that squeezes through the gaps in the traffic.*

(8) *Watch out for motorbikes and cyclists when turning left.*

(10) *Bikes are small and hard to see. Look twice and be sure.*

On your driving test, the examiner will be looking to see how well you judge what others using the road are going to do, and whether you react safely. Pay particular attention to the most vulnerable road users – pedestrians, cyclists and motorcyclists.

Slow down anywhere near children who are playing, and take extra care near schools (1).

Drive slowly past ice cream vans and look carefully for the child

Bear in mind that bikes are small and hard to see. Look twice and be sure (10).

So remember to concentrate all the time that you are driving. Make use of the road signs and road markings to assess what lies ahead. Look all around for possible problems and reduce speed when your vision is restricted or when your space is reduced.

That way, you will avoid accidents, stay safe, and give

your passengers a comfortable and confident drive. Don't forget that when you take your driving test, the examiner is your passenger. By giving him a comfortable ride that avoids harsh or late braking, you demonstrate that you are fully in control and that you are anticipating problems in good time. As a result, your chances of passing the test increase enormously.

The Highway Code

Whenever you drive, you are expected to follow the rules and advice given in the Highway Code.

Please do not make the mistake of thinking that these rules and commonsense pieces of advice are only for learner drivers. They are designed to help you stay safe and avoid accidents long after you have forgotten that you ever took a test.

On your driving test, the examiner will expect to see you put the Highway Code into practice all the time that you are driving.

At the end of the test the examiner will ask you some questions about the rules, and get you to identify some signs and road markings. He may ask a question which relates to something that happened while you were driving.

For example, say that when you turned a corner, you did not give way to some pedestrians who were crossing the road. The incident itself may not have been dangerous, but the examiner will want to find out whether you know the rule. He may ask 'When you are turning into a side road, what would you be looking for and what actions would you take on what you saw?' If in your answer you state that you should give way to pedestrians who are crossing, the examiner may give you the benefit of the doubt about what happened when you were driving.

Examiners carry with them a flip-book which contains pictures of the main signs, signals and road markings. You will be asked to name some of them, and they may relate to signs you should have spotted on the drive. You will be expected to identify most of them correctly.

The next four pages contain a selection of signs. They all show a picture of somewhere you might expect to find the sign, together with three possible answers, only one of which is correct. Tick the box provided for the answer you think is correct in each case. Remember, though, that the whole Highway Code is not covered here. It is essential that you know the entire Code, as the examiner may well choose different questions.

To help you to get the right answers, here are the keys to the signing system:

• Circles give orders, eg: 'No right turn' or 'You must turn right ahead'.

• Triangles warn, eg: 'Roadworks'.

• Rectangles inform, eg: 'Hospital'.

Have a go at the questions. The answers are on page 77.

 a. minimum speed

b. maximum speed ✓

(1) c. recommended speed limit

 a. turn left ahead

b. turn left ✓

(2) c. keep left

 a. priority ahead

b. crossroads ✓

(3) c. church steeple

 a. use both lanes

b. no overtaking ✓

(4) c. no motor vehicles

 a. bend to the right ✓

b. sharp deviation of route to right

(5) c. diversion ahead, turn right

 a. end of dual carriageway

b. single line traffic ahead

(6) c. road narrows on both sides ✓

 a. turn left ahead ✓

b. turn left

(7) c. one-way street to the left

 a. no through road ✓

b. telephone kiosk

(8) c. road closed

a. sharp deviation of route to right ✓

b. sharp temporary deviation of route to right

(9) c. road closed

 a. hump bridge

b. uneven road ✓

(10) c. road subsidence

a. waiting restrictions

b. end of restriction

(11) c. national speed limit applies ✓

 a. ahead only ✓

b. one-way traffic

(12) c. one lane only ahead

 a. no entry

b. no vehicles

(13) c. no entry for vehicular traffic ✓

 a. automatic half barrier
level crossing

b. level crossing with no gates ✓

(14) c. disused level crossing

 a. ahead only

b. one-way street ✓

(15) c. dual carriageway ahead

 a. narrow vehicles only

b. no large vehicles

(16) c. no vehicles over width shown ✓

 a. road narrows on both sides

b. roads merge ahead

(17) c. dual carriageway ends ✓

 a. steep hill downwards ✓

b. steep hill upwards

(18) c. height limit

 a. cyclists only

b. recommended route for cyclists

(19) c. no cycling

 a. roundabout

b. mini-roundabout

(20) c. anti-clockwise one-way system

 ✓

 a. turn left

b. keep left

(21) c. turn left ahead

✓

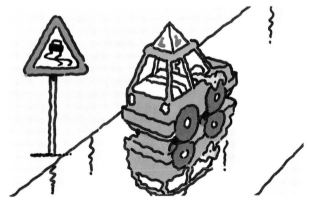

 a. contra-flow bus and cycle lane

b. with-flow bus and cycle lane

(22) c. buses and cyclists prohibited

 ✓

 a. deviation to the left

b. slippery road

(23) c. cars skidding ahead

✓

 a. pedestrians only

b. pedestrians crossing

(24) c. no pedestrians

 ✓

Picture questions

This section, which consists of a series of picture questions, is designed to test your knowledge of the rules in the Highway Code and of 'other motoring matters' which relate to your safety on the road. At the end of the driving test your examiner may ask you questions similar to those given on the following pages.

It seems likely that over the next couple of years, the questions asked may be drawn from a greater variety of topics, and that more importance may be placed on correct answers. By 1992, we may be obliged to make our driving test conform to EC standards. Eventually we may have a written paper as well as a practical test. In the meantime, it is reasonably certain that the oral questions will form an increasingly important part of our current driving test.

Subjects included in this section are: junctions, roundabouts, positioning, overtaking, parking, level crossings, motorways and other motoring matters.

In some of the pictures there are several vehicles and a number of streets. Each vehicle is numbered and each street is given a letter. With each picture is a series of questions or statements requiring either a Yes/No or True/False answer. Study the picture and answer each question by placing a tick in the space provided.

Please note:

• In some questions, it may help to turn the book on its side or upside-down to view the picture as though you were the driver of the vehicle concerned.

• The drawings are not to scale.

• They do not show everything you would see in a real-life situation. To make the drawings easier to study, only things which are relevant to the question have been included.

Answers

Short explanations are given with the correct answers on pages 78 and 79. If your answer is wrong, study the picture again and re-read the question carefully. Make sure you understand the reason for the answer provided.

Have fun!

Junctions

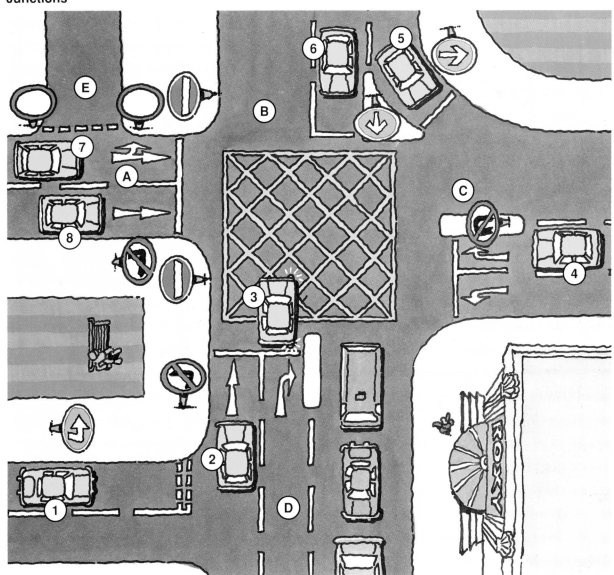

1) May vehicle 1 turn right at road D? . . . . NO

2) May vehicle 2 turn left into road A? . . . . NO

3) Should vehicle 3 have entered box junction to turn into road C? . . . . YES

4) May vehicle 4 make a U-turn back along road C? . . . . NO

5) May vehicle 5 turn left into road C? . . . . YES

6) May vehicle 6 turn left into road C?. . . . . NO

7) May vehicle 6 enter box junction to go ahead into road D?. . . . . NO

8) May vehicle 7 turn left into road E?. . . . . NO

9) May vehicle 7 turn left into road B?. . . . . YES

10) May vehicle 8 turn right into road D?. . . . . NO

Roundabouts

<table>
<tr><td></td><td></td><td colspan="2">YES/NO</td></tr>
<tr><td>1)</td><td>Should vehicle 1 give way to vehicle 2?</td><td>✓</td><td></td></tr>
<tr><td>2)</td><td>Should vehicle 3 give way to vehicle 4?</td><td></td><td>✓</td></tr>
<tr><td>3)</td><td>Should vehicle 5 signal left here if taking road B?</td><td>✓</td><td></td></tr>
<tr><td>4)</td><td>Should vehicle 6 signal right here if taking road D?</td><td>✓</td><td></td></tr>
<tr><td>5)</td><td>Should vehicle 5 take the blue line if taking road C?</td><td></td><td>✓</td></tr>
<tr><td>6)</td><td>Should vehicle 2 signal left here if taking road D?</td><td>✓</td><td></td></tr>
<tr><td>7)</td><td>Should vehicle 7 take the blue line to reach road F?</td><td></td><td>✓</td></tr>
<tr><td>8)</td><td>Should vehicle 8 signal here if taking road D?</td><td></td><td>✓</td></tr>
<tr><td>9)</td><td>Should vehicle 9 signal if taking road G?</td><td></td><td>✓</td></tr>
<tr><td>10)</td><td>Should vehicle 10 overtake vehicle 11?</td><td></td><td>✓</td></tr>
</table>

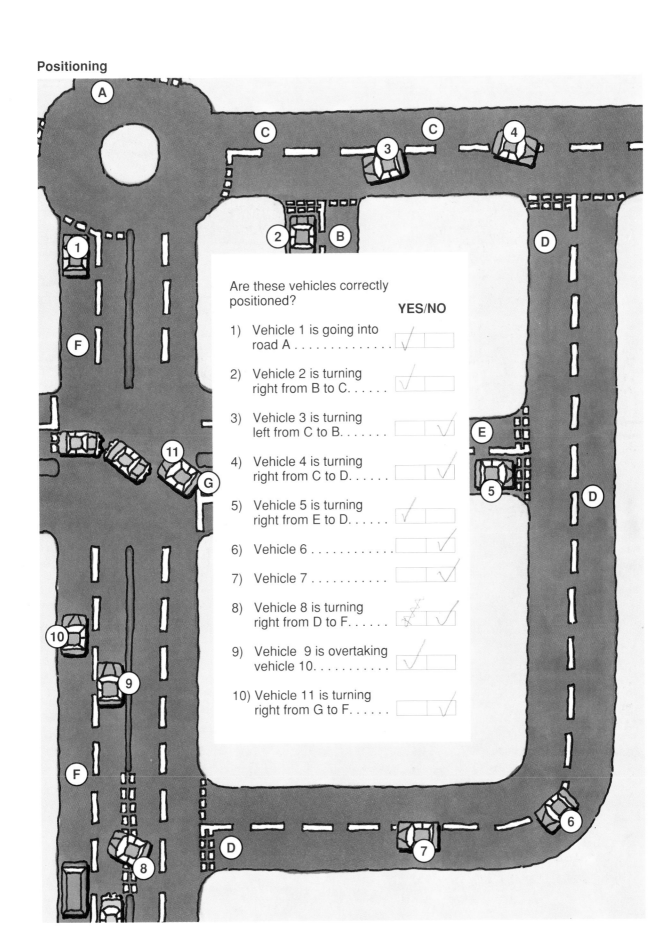

Are these vehicles correctly positioned?

YES/NO

1) Vehicle 1 is going into road A . . . . ☑ ☐

2) Vehicle 2 is turning right from B to C. . . . . . ☑ ☐

3) Vehicle 3 is turning left from C to B. . . . . . . ☐ ☑

4) Vehicle 4 is turning right from C to D. . . . . . ☐ ☑

5) Vehicle 5 is turning right from E to D. . . . . . ☑ ☐

6) Vehicle 6 . . . . ☐ ☑

7) Vehicle 7 . . . . ☐ ☑

8) Vehicle 8 is turning right from D to F. . . . . . ☐ ☑

9) Vehicle 9 is overtaking vehicle 10. . . . . ☑ ☐

10) Vehicle 11 is turning right from G to F. . . . . . ☐ ☑

Overtaking

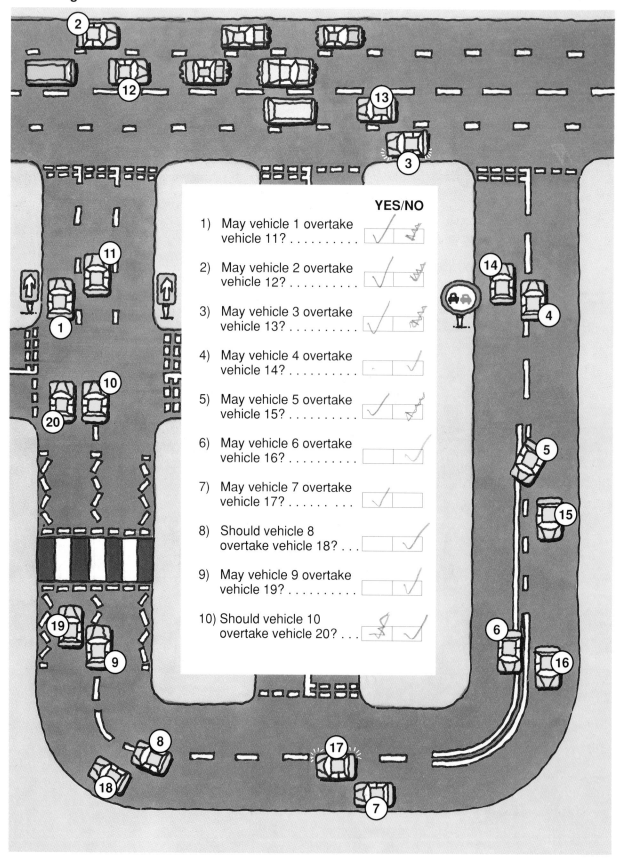

YES/NO

1) May vehicle 1 overtake vehicle 11? . . . . ✓

2) May vehicle 2 overtake vehicle 12? . . . . ✓

3) May vehicle 3 overtake vehicle 13? . . . . ✓

4) May vehicle 4 overtake vehicle 14? . . . . ✓

5) May vehicle 5 overtake vehicle 15? . . . . ✓

6) May vehicle 6 overtake vehicle 16? . . . . ✓

7) May vehicle 7 overtake vehicle 17? . . . . ✓

8) Should vehicle 8 overtake vehicle 18? . . . ✓

9) May vehicle 9 overtake vehicle 19? . . . . ✓

10) Should vehicle 10 overtake vehicle 20? . . . ✓

Parking

Look at the picture above, then tick yes or no according to whether you think the vehicle is correctly parked.

YES/NO

Vehicle 1 . . . .

Vehicle 2 . . . .

Vehicle 3 . . . .

Vehicle 4 . . . .

Vehicle 5 . . . .

Vehicle 6 . . . .

Vehicle 7 . . . .

Vehicle 8 . . . .

Vehicle 9 . . . .

Vehicle 10 . . . .

Level crossings

1) After the amber lights flash and the alarm sounds, the barriers come down. . . . .

2) Drivers of large or slow vehicles must phone the signalman and get permission to cross.

3) If you stall or break down on the crossing, get your passengers to help push your vehicle clear. . . . .

4) Some crossings with lights do not have barriers. . . . .

5) If the barriers stay down and the lights continue to flash, it means another train is coming

6) If, after about 3 minutes, the barriers stay down, you may zig-zag around them. . . . .

7) You should not enter the yellow box unless there is enough clear road beyond the crossing for your vehicle. . . . .

8) If you do telephone the signalman before crossing, phone again afterwards to let him know you are over. . . . .

9) Red flashing lights mean stop. . . . .

10) Always give way to trains. . . . .

Motorways

1) May vehicle 1 join the motorway? . . . .

2) Is vehicle 2 (a pedal cycle) allowed on a motorway? . . . .

3) Is vehicle 3 (a 250cc motorcycle) allowed on a motorway? . . . .

4) May vehicle 4 use the gap in the central reservation to make a U-turn? . . . .

5) May vehicle 5 park here? . . . .

6) Will vehicle 6 need to move to the middle lane ahead? . . . .

7) Should vehicle 7 move to the left-hand lane. (There are no vehicles ahead.) . . . .

8) May vehicle 8 (a coach) use the right-hand lane of a three-lane motorway? . . . .

9) May vehicle 9 (a heavy goods vehicle) use the right-hand lane of a three-lane motorway?

10) May vehicle 10 reverse up the hard shoulder to take the exit slip road that it has missed?

Other motoring matters

1) In very heavy rain, a car's tyres may ride up on top of the surface water. This is called aquaplaning.

TRUE	✓
FALSE	

2) It is illegal to set off with windows that are iced up.

TRUE	✓
FALSE	

3) In thick fog, it is a good idea to try to keep the rear lights of the vehicle in front of you in your view.

TRUE	
FALSE	✓

4) When moving off in ice or snow, use a higher gear to get more grip.

TRUE	✓
FALSE	

5) If your vehicle skids like this, you need to come off the brake first, and then steer right to straighten the car.

TRUE	✓
FALSE	

6)   A driver can tell his tyre pressures are too low because the steering will feel heavy.

TRUE	✓
FALSE	

7)   Switch your lights on as late as possible to prevent draining the battery.

TRUE	
FALSE	✓

8)   If you break down on an ordinary road, you should place a warning triangle at least 50 metres behind your car.

TRUE	✓
FALSE	

9)   After driving through a ford or flooded road, a driver should dry his brakes by using his left foot to apply the brake while accelerating gently with the right foot.

TRUE	✓
FALSE	

10)   You should not use a hand-held telephone when your vehicle is moving, except in an emergency.

TRUE	✓
FALSE	

Quiz

As a further test of your general motoring knowledge, try answering the 20 questions below and see how you score. Again, they are all examples of the type of question your examiner may well ask you at the end of your test. Each one gives you three choices of answer. Only one answer – a, b, or c – is correct. Tick the box provided for the answer you think is correct. When you have answered all 20 questions, check your answers by looking at page 77.

1. You should check the pressures of your tyres when they are:
   a. hot. ☐
   b. cold. ☑
   c. warm. ☐

2. You notice that your tyres are worn mainly on the outside edges. This is likely to have been caused by:
   a. under-inflation of the tyres. ☑
   b. over-inflation of the tyres. ☐
   c. old age. ☐

3. If you inflate your tyres above their recommended pressures, this is likely to cause:
   a. the steering to feel heavier. ☐
   b. their grip with the road to be reduced. ☑
   c. them to overheat. ☐

4. If you fit a mixture of radial and cross-ply tyres to your car, the radials must be fitted:
   a. on both back wheels only. ☑
   b. on both front wheels only. ☐
   c. on one front and one back wheel on opposite sides of the car. ☐

5. If you see that the tyres of your car are worn badly in the centre of their tread pattern, it is most likely that:
   a. there is too much pressure in the tyres. ☑
   b. there is too little pressure in the tyres. ☐
   c. this is a normal pattern of wear. ☐

6. The minimum legal tread depth across the width of the tread of a vehicle tyre must be:
   a. 1mm. ☐
   b. 1.6mm. ☑
   c. 2mm. ☐

7. If you apply the brakes and cause your wheels to lock, you should:
   a. put the handbrake on and pump the footbrake. ☐
   b. brake harder and change to a lower gear. ☐
   c. take your foot off the brake and reapply the brake more gently. ☑

8. When you push the brake pedal, it feels 'spongy'. It is likely that:
   a. the brakes need adjusting. ☐
   b. the brakes need relining. ☐
   c. there is air in the hydraulic system. ☑

9. After a long spell of dry weather, a road is likely to be most slippery when it has:
   a. just started to rain. ☑
   b. been raining for some considerable time. ☐
   c. just stopped raining. ☐

10. To correct a skid where

the rear wheels of your car are sliding to the right, you should:

a. steer to the left. ☐

b. steer to the right. ☑

c. not turn the steering wheel. ☐

11. After driving through a flood, you should immediately check:

a. for water in the distributor. ☐

b. for water in the dynamo. ☐

c. your brakes. ☑

12. When you park your car facing uphill and parallel to the nearside kerb, you should leave it with the front wheels turned:

a. to the left. ☐

b. to the right. ☑

c. straight ahead. ☐

13. When you park your car facing downhill, you should leave it with the front wheels turned:

a. towards the kerb. ☑

b. away from the kerb. ☐

c. straight ahead. ☐

14. Bus lanes operate for periods shown by the time plates. Outside these times, a bus lane may be used by:

a. cyclists only. ☐

b. coaches and goods vehicles only. ☐

c. all vehicles. ☑

15. While driving round a bend, you notice that your oil warning light flickers. This is likely to indicate that:

a. the oil pump has broken. ☐

b. the level of oil in the sump is very low. ☑

c. the level of oil in the sump is between maximum and minimum. ☐

16. While driving along an open road, you notice that the temperature gauge of your car is rising rapidly. This is most likely to mean that:

a. the engine oil is low. ☐

b. the spark plugs are oiled up. ☐

c. the fan belt has broken. ☑

17. While driving along normally, you see the ignition warning light come on. The most likely reason is that:

a. the distributor cap has broken. ☐

b. the fan belt has broken. ☑

c. the battery is overcharging. ☐

18. The MOT test regulations require that all cars must be tested once a year if they are, from their date of registration:

a. over two years old. ☐

b. over one year old. ☑

c. over three years old. ☑

19. If you are required by the police to produce an MOT vehicle test certificate for inspection, you may do so at a police station of your choice within:

a. 3 days. ☐

b. 5 days. ☐

c. 7 days. ☑

20. A person aged 21 years old who has just passed the L-test is legally allowed to supervise a learner driver of the same licence group on the public road:

a. immediately. ☐

b. after three years. ☑

c. once the full licence has been received. ☐

After the test

At the end of the driving test, the examiner will tell you whether you have passed or failed. If you study this book carefully and only take your test when your instructor tells you that you are ready, then you should have little trouble passing at the first attempt.

When you pass your driving test, your examiner will ask you for your driving licence, and will issue you with a Certificate of Competence and ask you to sign it. You should send this certificate to DVLC Swansea when you apply for your full licence.

If you fail, the examiner will give you a Statement of Failure (Form DL24) on which he has marked the most serious faults you have committed during the test, and he may also spend a few moments discussing these with you. He will not mark down every fault that you made.

When the test is over, always discuss the faults marked with your instructor. He has been trained to interpret a Statement of Failure and will be able to explain where you went wrong.

Don't give up. You cannot take another test in the same class of vehicle for at least one calendar month, but you should apply for another test date immediately. Remember that every Test Centre will have a waiting list of people wishing to take tests. This will vary from one Test Centre to the next, but

is never likely to be less than five or six weeks.

It is best not to leave a gap before continuing your lessons and practice sessions. The longer you wait, the more you will slip back, so follow your instructor's advice and book a course of lessons to take you up to your next test.

Remember, the examiner has only pointed out your most serious faults. Do not make the mistake of only practising those. You are likely to find that you fail on a different item the next time if you do.

However, if you have been successful you are now legally entitled to remove your 'L' plates and drive your vehicle on your own, without any supervision.

Don't drive away from the Test Centre yourself. Let your instructor drive for you. You will probably be far too excited to concentrate.

Driving on your own
You are likely to find that driving on your own is both exciting and a little nerve-racking at first. If you keep practising the skills you have been taught, you should find that your ability to control your car improves very quickly. Please be careful, because it is easy to develop a false sense of security. You no longer stall, or have problems steering and so on. Everything seems to come naturally, without your having to

think about it. So it can be all too easy to think that this alone has made you a good driver. But if your ability to look, spot problems early, assess risks and act sensibly does not also develop, you are likely to get caught out. Many people have an accident within the first year of driving.

For your own safety and that of others, you are strongly advised to work towards taking an advanced driving test. There is no legal requirement to do so, which many people argue is wrong. But a voluntary test does have some advantages, not least that the tuition and the test itself can be conducted in a more friendly and informal way. Most people who have taken these tests have found the experience both pleasant and rewarding. There are two organisations that conduct advanced driving tests, the Institute of Advanced Motorists, and the Royal Society for the Prevention of Accidents. The addresses from which you can obtain information are given on page 77 of this book. Your local British School of Motoring branch will be pleased to explain these advanced tests in more detail, and to give advice to you about the tuition you need to achieve the required standard.

Motorways

(1) *You will normally join at a roundabout.*

Motorways are designed to carry multiple lanes of traffic at high speed in as direct a route as possible between major cities. They may not be used by learner drivers. Although they are the safest of all our roads, tragic accidents can occur through a momentary slip in concentration. The British School of Motoring advises that every person who passes a learner driver test should obtain professional tuition in motorway driving. We believe that this is essential if road safety is to improve, as one day it could save your life – or that of someone else.

Safe motorway driving starts before you set out:

• YOU need to be fit, alert and well rested.

• YOUR CAR needs to be in good condition.

• THE ROUTE needs planning. You need to know where you will join and leave the motorway, and where there are service areas to allow you to break a long journey.

Checking road and weather reports before you set off can save you hours of delay and frustration.

Joining a motorway

You will normally join at a roundabout (1). Make sure you go the right way. If you take the wrong slip road, you cannot simply reverse or turn around.

(2) *Look for a gap, and give a signal.*

(3) *Steer gently into the left-hand lane and cancel your signal.*

You will be forced to go on to the next exit and come back.

The slip road normally goes downhill into an acceleration lane which runs alongside the main carriageway.

Keep plenty of space between you and other traffic.

Give yourself time to look for a gap in the through traffic already on the motorway (2). Give a signal so that everyone can see you.

Some drivers may move over to the middle lane to let you in. When you see a gap, increase your speed to match the through traffic. Try not to cause them to slow down when you join.

Steer gently into the left-hand lane and cancel your signal (3). Stay in the left-hand lane while you get used to the higher speed.

Speed

Your speed on a motorway is very deceptive, so check your speedometer regularly (4).

(4) *Check your speedometer regularly.*

Take regular looks in your mirrors (5). Your first glance may show a tiny speck in the distance. With a second glance, you may find that the car is almost on top of you.

(5) *Take regular looks in your mirrors.*

Flashing speed-limit signs are advisory (6). Follow the advice. There may be lane closures or stationary traffic queues ahead.

A statutory round sign (7) is compulsory, and you must obey it. Major roadworks have these signs. There may be two-way traffic using one carriageway. This is called a contra-flow system.

(6) *This type of sign is advisory.*

Keep your distance

A two-vehicle collision becomes a multiple pile-up because drivers don't leave a safety gap between them and the vehicle in front (8).

Use the 'two-second' rule (9). When the vehicle ahead goes under a bridge or past a sign, start counting, 'one thousand and one, one thousand and two'. If you reach the same point before you have finished counting, you are too close. Drop back a little and count again. Remember in bad weather you need at least to double the distance.

Driving in lanes

You should drive in the left-hand lane unless you are overtaking.

(7) *This type of sign is compulsory.*

On a three-lane motorway, you may stay in the middle lane if you are overtaking a number of slower-moving vehicles. Do not weave in and out.

The right-hand lane is for overtaking only (10). You must return to the middle lane as soon as possible after overtaking.

(8) *A two-vehicle collision becomes a multiple pile-up because drivers don't leave a safety gap between them and the vehicle in front.*

(9) *Use the 'two-second' rule.*

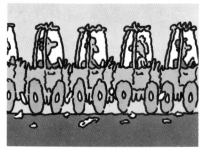

(10) *The right-hand lane is for overtaking only.*

Keep a check for faster moving traffic coming up behind (11). Let them through as soon as you can, even if they are breaking the speed limit.

Changing lanes

Look well ahead for reasons why you might need to change lanes:

• Slow moving traffic (12).

• Vehicles joining at a junction (13).

Don't leave changing lanes to the last moment. Check behind for a suitable gap and signal before moving out.

Check visually over your shoulder to see if another driver is alongside hidden in your blind spot (14).

Steer gently into the new lane (15). Sudden movements can cause loss of control.

Remember to cancel your signal and check the new situation behind. Only make one lane change at a time.

Overtaking

The rules for overtaking are essentially the same as on ordinary roads.

Overtake only on the right, unless traffic is moving in queues, and the left-hand lane is moving faster (16).

Otherwise, NEVER move to a lane on the left in order to overtake.

Before you overtake, look in your mirrors and decide if the vehicles behind are catching you up. Look

(14) *Glance over your shoulder to see if another driver is alongside, hidden in your blind spot.*

(15) *Steer gently into the new lane.*

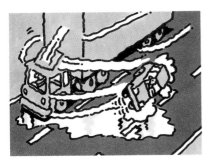

(11) *Keep checking for fast moving traffic coming up behind.*

(12) *Slow moving traffic should remain in the left-hand lane.*

(13) *Vehicles joining at a junction.*

(16) *Overtake only on the right, unless traffic is moving in queues and the left-hand lane is moving faster.*

(17) *Avoid driving three abreast, and do not rely on other drivers to check before they move out.*

more than once to help you judge their speed. Ask yourself if you can get out and past before they reach you.

Avoid driving three abreast (17), and remember that you cannot rely on other drivers to check before moving out.

Wait until the vehicle you are overtaking appears in your interior mirror before moving back to the left (18).

Leaving the motorway

By keeping track of each exit as you go along, you will know when the next one is yours.

The first indication you will see is the one-mile sign, which has your exit number on it (19). Look well ahead and decide whether you have time to overtake any slow moving vehicles before you reach the half-mile sign.

By the time you reach this sign, you should be in the left-hand lane. Adjust your speed to keep a safe distance from traffic in front.

The countdown markers start 300 yards from the exit, and are 100 yards apart. Start to signal between the 300 and 200 yard markers (20).

Check for other drivers leaving the motorway who may cut in at the last moment (21).

Steer gently into the deceleration lane and start to reduce speed. Check your speedometer and

reduce speed to go safely past any sharp bends or junctions ahead.

Give yourself time to adjust to ordinary roads again, and remember that you will feel as though you are driving more slowly than you really are. Check your speedometer to be sure.

(19) *The first indication you will see that your exit is coming up is the one-mile sign, which has the exit number on it.*

(20) *Start to signal between the 300 and 200-yard markers.*

(18) *Wait until the vehicle you are overtaking appears in your interior mirror before moving back to the left.*

(21) *Check for other drivers leaving the motorway who may cut in at the last moment.*

Roadworks

When you see roadwork signs, get into lane early, obey the speed limits and be patient (22).

Watch out for others cutting in at the last moment (23).

Breakdowns

If you break down, try to get over to the hard shoulder and stop as far to the left as you can. Get out of the passenger door.

Marker posts direct you to the nearest phone (24), which will connect you to the police control unit. You are strongly advised to become a member of a breakdown organisation, whose services will help to keep inconvenience and delay to a minimum.

Bad weather

In bad weather, slow down and make sure you really can stop in the distance you can see to be clear.

Allow a bigger gap. You may need as much as ten times the usual distance to stop on ice.

Make sure others can see you by switching on your headlights. Only use rear fog lamps if visibility is down to less than 100 metres.

Services

Services allow you to break up your motorway journey. Driving along a motorway is very tiring and requires a high level of concentration.

A 15-minute break every two hours is essential for safety on long journeys (25). The whole family gets a break from the car. Your car cools down, and so do you and your passengers.

Remember, until you pass your driving test, you are not allowed to drive on a motorway. Many of you will travel down a motorway as a passenger between now and then. You will find it helpful to start looking at the way other drivers behave. Try using the two-second rule, both for the car in which you are travelling and also by noting the safety gap that other drivers keep in relation to their speed. Look out for drivers who break the rules and ask yourself whether you will become another risk-taker, or whether you will learn to cope with this situation by receiving expert tuition.

In July 1991, The British School of Motoring, in conjunction with the Road Transport Industry Training Board, introduced a new voluntary Motorway Driving Test. A team of specially trained examiners are available to assess both your knowledge and your skill and to give advice in a friendly and informal manner. Gold, silver and bronze certificates are awarded according to your level of ability. Further information about this test can be obtained from your local BSM branch.

(22) *When you see the signs, get into lane early, obey the speed limits and be patient.*

(23) *Watch out for other drivers cutting in at the last moment.*

(24) *Marker posts direct you to the nearest emergency phone, which will connect you to the police control unit.*

(25) *The whole family gets a break from the car. Your car cools down, and so do you and your passengers.*

Night driving

(1) *Use headlights, even in town.*

(2) *On an unlit road, headlights on full beam allow you to see about 100 metres ahead.*

(3) *On an unlit road, dipped headlights allow you to see about 40 metres ahead.*

Driving tests only take place during the hours of daylight, and many learner drivers will pass the test never having had a lesson or any practice in the dark. The chances of being involved in an accident are greater in the dark than in daylight. You cannot see as far or as much at night, and you receive far less information about your surroundings. It is harder to judge both speed and distance, and driving is more of a strain, particularly on the eyes. From dusk to dawn you must rely on lights to see and be seen.

Preparing for your journey

Driving at night is a great strain on your eyes. As you get older, your eyesight may alter. Such changes tend to take place so gradually that you are unlikely to notice them. The only way you can be sure your vision is adequate is to have your eyesight checked regularly, preferably by visiting a qualified optician.

Don't use tinted glasses or sun-glasses at night. They reduce your vision.

Keep your windscreen clean. You will see better and be less dazzled by other vehicles' lights.

Check that all your lights are working, and that they are clean and properly adjusted. The effectiveness of your lights is greatly reduced if they are dirty.

If you are too tired, don't drive.

Driving safely in the dark

See and be seen.

It is best to use headlights on all roads, even in town where there is street lighting (1). Sidelights alone are not enough, and make it difficult for other drivers and pedestrians to see that you are there.

At dusk, be the first to turn on your lights. At dawn, be the last to turn them off.

Speed and visibility

You should be able to stop well within the limits of your lighting. On an unlit road, headlights on full beam allow you to see about 100 metres ahead (2).

On an unlit road, dipped headlights allow you to see about 40 metres ahead (3).

Pedestrians and cyclists are hard to see in the dark (4).

Cats' eyes help you follow the course of the road ahead (5).

(4) *Pedestrians and cyclists are hard to see in the dark.*

Meeting other vehicles

The lights of another vehicle usually tell you its direction of travel, but little about its speed.

Decide if you need to slow down, and look for any obstructions in the road ahead.

Dip your headlights to avoid dazzling oncoming drivers . Do not dip so soon that you cannot see the road ahead.

Do not stare at the oncoming headlights, but look slightly towards the left-hand edge of your dipped beams. Be ready to stop if necessary.

Dip your lights earlier when going round a left-hand bend. Your headlight beams will sweep across the eyes of anyone coming towards you.
If an oncoming driver fails to dip his lights and dazzles you, slow down and stop if necessary (6).

Following other vehicles at night

Do not dazzle the driver in front. Dip your lights, and keep far enough back that your dipped beams fall clear of his rear window.

Overtaking at night

Extra care is needed, because it is much harder to judge space and distance and the speed of other vehicles at night. Dangers are far more likely to be hidden from view in the dark.

You cannot see properly beyond the range of your headlights.

Bends or dips in the road may conceal parked or approaching vehicles (7).

Cyclists and pedestrians may be hidden in the gloom.

Warning of your presence at night

Flash your headlights if necessary to warn of your presence. It is illegal to use your horn when driving in a built-up area between the hours of 11.30pm and 7.00am (8).

(6) If an oncoming driver fails to dip his lights and dazzles you, slow down and stop if necessary.

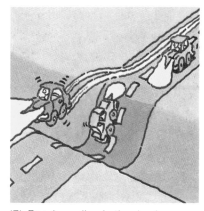

(7) Bends or dips in the road may conceal parked or approaching vehicles.

(5) Cats' eyes help you follow the course of the road ahead.

(8) It is illegal to use your horn in a built-up area between 11.30pm and 7.00am.

You and your car

(1) *P - is for petrol.*

(2) *O - is for oil.*

(3) *W - is for water.*

Once you have passed your driving test and possess your own car, you will become responsible for making sure that it is properly taxed, insured and tested. Most people do not start their driving career by buying a brand new car. They are far more likely to buy a secondhand one, and care is needed to ensure that what they buy is a sensible purchase in relation to the price they can afford. Unless you have mechanical knowledge, it is worth paying an expert to assess your intended purchase. Some motoring organisations offer this service, which can save you much worry and helps take the risk out of buying secondhand.

You will then need to ensure that your car is always in a good roadworthy condition. Many people have a fear of breaking down. You can reduce this risk enormously, if you follow the advice given below.

Always read your car handbook, and stick to the manufacturers' recommendations.

Have your car serviced at regular intervals and keep a record of any work done.

Daily checks
Walk round your car and look for obvious problems, flat tyres, damage to lights, loose trim, etc.

Make sure everything carried in the car is secure, and put loose items in the boot or glove compartment.

(4) *E - is for electrics.*

(5) *R - is for rubber.*

Make sure the windscreen and windows are clean.

After you drive off, check that your brakes are working properly as soon as you safely can.

Weekly checks
Think of the word POWER, to help you remember what you should check:

• **P** - is for petrol (or diesel)(1). Make sure you have enough fuel for your journey. Allow extra in case you get caught in a traffic jam.

- **O** - is for oil (2). Check the oil level and top it up if necessary. Check the brake fluid level, and also the clutch fluid, which may be in a separate container. If the oil pressure or brake warning lights come on while you are driving, stop as soon as you safely can and get help.

- **W** - is for water (3). Check the radiator, or expansion tank, for the coolant level. Do this when the engine is cold. If it is hot, scalding water may spray over you as you remove the cap. Top up the windscreen washer bottle(s).

- **E** - is for electrics (4). Make sure all the lights and indicators are working. Get someone to help you check the brake lights. Keep spare bulbs in the car, so that you can carry out a quick roadside repair. (If you take your car abroad, this is usually a legal requirement.) Check that the battery connections are tight and clean. Top up the battery with distilled water if necessary.

- **R** - is for rubber (5). Make sure your tyre treads are well above the minimum legal limit, and that there are no cuts or bulges in them. Check the tyre pressures when they are cold. Remember to check the spare.

Make sure the fan belt is tight and not worn.

Check the wiper blades, and replace them if they start smearing the windscreen.

Most car breakdowns are the result of failing to follow these simple steps.

If you do break down, membership in a breakdown organisation will take much of the worry and strain out of the misery.

Useful addresses

The following are the key organisations most likely to be of use to the general motorist.

The British School of Motoring Ltd
81-87 Hartfield Road
London SW19 3TJ
(Tel 081 540 8262)

Driver and Vehicle Licensing Centre (DVLC)
Swansea SA99 1AN
(Tel 0792 72134)

The Driving Standards Agency
Stanley House
Talbot Street
Nottingham NG1 5GU
(Tel 0602 474222)

Institute of Advanced Motorists (IAM)
IAM House
359-365 Chiswick High Road
London W4 4HS
(Tel 081 994 4403)

Royal Automobile Club (RAC)
PO Box 100
RAC House
Lansdowne Road
Croydon CR9 2JA
(Tel 081 686 2525)

Royal Society for the Prevention of Accidents
Cannon House
Priory Queensway
Birmingham
(Tel 021 233 2461)

The Highway Code

1. b	4. b	7. a	10. b	13. c	16. c	19. b	22. b
2. b	5. a	8. a	11. c	14. b	17. c	20. b	23. b
3. b	6. c	9. a	12. b	15. a	18. a	21. b	24. c

Quiz answers

1. b	4. a	7. c	10. b	13. a	16. c	19. c
2. a	5. a	8. c	11. c	14. c	17. b	20. b
3. b	6. b	9. a	12. b	15. b	18. c	

Answers and explanations

Junctions (page 57)

1) No.
The compulsory 'left turn ahead' sign prohibits this.

2) No.
The 'no left turn' and 'no entry' signs prohibit this.

3) Yes.
Because vehicle 3's exit into road C is clear.

4) No.
The 'no U-turn' sign prohibits this.

5) Yes.
It is a compulsory left turn in the lane that vehicle 5 is in.

6) No.
The sign 'ahead only' prohibits turning left or right.

7) No.
Vehicle 6's exit into road D is blocked by traffic, so it may not enter the yellow box.

8) No.
The sign 'no vehicles' prohibits this.

9) Yes.
There is no sign to prohibit this.

10) No.
The 'no right turn' sign prohibits this.

Roundabouts (page 58)

1) Yes.
The general rule at roundabouts is give way to traffic from the right on the roundabout.

2) No.
The road marking indicates that vehicle 4 should give way. In this situation vehicle 4 gives way in the roundabout.

3) Yes.
Vehicle 5 should signal left on the approach and through the roundabout.

4) Yes.
Vehicle 6 should signal right on the approach and change to a left signal when it reaches the position of vehicle 2.

5) No.
Vehicle 5 should keep to the left through the roundabout. This would allow vehicle 6 to take the inside route for turning right.

6) Yes.
Signal left when passing the exit before the one you want to take.

7) No.
Even if the disc is only a mini-roundabout painted on the road, vehicle 7 should try to go around it.

8) No.
Vehicle 8 is going straight over, so should only signal as it passes road F, if at all.

9) No.
A right signal might make others think vehicle 9 was going where vehicle 4 is. A left-turn signal would be taken to mean going into road F. To avoid misleading signals, it would be safer not to signal.

10) No.
Long vehicles may need all the available space to negotiate the roundabout.

Positioning (page 59)

1) Yes.
The left lane is correct for going straight ahead at roundabouts with two lanes on the approach.

2) Yes.
You should keep well to the left when turning right out of narrow side roads. This leaves room for vehicles turning in.

3) No.
Vehicle 3 should be closer to the kerb in order not to mislead other road users.

4) No.
Vehicle 4 is already over the centre line, thus blocking oncoming traffic.

5) Yes.
Road E is a one-way street, because the 'give way' lines go right across the road.

6) No.
Vehicle 6 is driving on the centre line, risking a head-on collision with a vehicle doing the same coming the other way.

7) No.
The rule is keep to the left, unless overtaking or turning right. Vehicle 7 is doing neither of those.

8) No.
Vehicle 8 should have waited in road D for both sides to be clear. There is not enough room to wait in the gap in the central reservation.

9) Yes.
Vehicle 9 is correctly positioned to overtake vehicle 10.

10) No.
Vehicle 11 should go around the back of the oncoming traffic.

Overtaking (page 60)

1) Yes.
In a one-way street, you may overtake on either side.

2) Yes.
When traffic is moving in queues, the left lane may move quicker than the right.

3) Yes.
If you are turning left, then you may overtake on the left.

4) No.
There is a 'no overtaking' sign which prohibits this.

5) Yes.
The broken white line is on vehicle 5's side of the road, so overtaking is permitted.

6) No.
Vehicle 6 is crossing a solid line to overtake; this is prohibited.

7) Yes.
Vehicle 7 may overtake on the left because vehicle 17 is indicating a right turn.

8) No.
Although not prohibited, it is not advisable to overtake on a bend.

9) No.
It is an offence to overtake the

leading vehicle when approaching a pedestrian crossing.

10) No.
Although not prohibited, it is not advisable to overtake at a road junction.

Parking (page 61)
Vehicle 1. No.
Blocking hospital entrance.

Vehicle 2. Yes.
The sign shows that pavement parking is permitted.

Vehicle 3. Yes.
The bus lane isn't operating at the time of the day shown on the clock.

Vehicle 4. No.
Parking is not permitted where there are double white lines in the middle of the road.

Vehicle 5. No.
Double yellow lines on the road mean waiting restrictions; the plate says 'no waiting' at any time.

Vehicle 6. No.
Parking at junctions makes it difficult for other road users to see each other.

Vehicle 7. Yes.
There are waiting restrictions, but not for the time of day shown.

Vehicle 8. No.
Not during the working day, unless a time plate states otherwise.

Vehicle 9. No.
Not on the pavement.

Vehicle 10. No.
It is an offence to park on the zig-zag lines at pedestrian crossings.

Level crossings (page 62)
1) False.
After the amber lights, red lights will flash, then the barriers will come down.

2) True.
Large means over 55 feet (16.8 metres) long or 9 feet 6 inches (2.9 metres) wide or 38 tonnes total weight. Slow means 5mph or less.

3) False.
Get everybody out of the vehicle and phone the signalman. Only then try to move the vehicle.

4) True.
An advance warning sign like this tells you there are no barriers.

5) True.
The lights will go out and the barriers go up when it is safe to cross.

6) False.
Never zig-zag around the barriers. Phone the signalman for advice.

7) True.
Never drive 'nose to tail' over crossings, just in case the traffic stops ahead, and you get stuck on the crossing.

8) True.

9) True.

10) True!

Motorways (page 63)
1) No.
The flashing red lights mean you must not enter the slip road.

2) No.

3) Yes.
Motorcycles over 50cc are allowed.

4) No.
U- turns are illegal on motorways.

5) No.
The hard shoulder is for emergencies and breakdowns only. You may park only at a service area.

6) Yes.
The sign indicates the right-hand lane is closed ahead.

7) Yes.
The rule 'keep to the left unless overtaking' applies to motorways as well as ordinary roads.

8) Yes.
Coaches and buses less than 12 metres (40 feet) in length may use the right-hand lane of a three-lane motorway.

9) No.
HGVs are restricted to the left and middle lanes of a three-lane motorway.

10) No.
You are not allowed to reverse on the motorway. If you miss your exit, you must go on to the next one.

Other motoring matters (pages 64 and 65)

1) True.

2) True.

3) False.
This may mean driving too close to the one in front.

4) True.

5) True.
If you don't come off the brakes first, you are likely to cause a skid in the other direction when you try to straighten up.

6) True.
The tyres, being softer, will stick to the road more. However, the car is less stable like this so it is not recommended.

7) False.
While you drive, the battery is being recharged. Put your lights on early so that others can see you.

8) True.

9) True.
Water in the brakes can affect their efficiency. Make sure they are working properly before building up speed again.

10) True.
You need your attention on the road and two hands on the wheel, just in case something goes wrong, such as a puncture.

Index